MW00528972

DNA of the Young Entrepreneur

A Way to Wealth for Young Entrepreneurs

By Sean McCauley

20660 Stevens Creek Blvd., Suite 210
Cupertino, CA 95014

First Printing: November 7, 2008
Paperback ISBN: 1-60005-122-7 (978-1-60005-122-7)
Place of Publication: Silicon Valley, California, USA
Paperback Library of Congress Number: 2008936652

eBook ISBN: 1-60005-124-3 (978-1-60005-124-1)

Trademarks

Warning and Disclaimer

Praise for this Book

"If you are at all serious about being successful in business the 'DNA of the Young Entrepreneur' is a must read! Sean McCauley has put together all of the elements needed to 'earn' your way to wealth. This is not only a practical guide, but a philosophical one. Calling on his own experience at an early age, he has detailed the route to success. You will never learn at business school what is presented in this book."
James P. Neeves, Retired Executive Vice President, W.R. Grace & Co.

"I've owned my own business for years, however for most of that time, my business owned me. Sean's book 'DNA of the Young Entrepreneur' has been a great tool to help me take control of my business again by following the same time management principles. How easy, now I have time to focus on where I really want my business to be. Thanks Sean! I can't wait for the next book."
Scott Ebert, My PC Partners

"'DNA of the Young Entrepreneur' is a book for the person seeking permission to be powerful and successful, regardless of their age. As I read through the principles, I think about my last few years as an entrepreneur and can attest that this is a must-read for anyone who is ready to embark on their journey, whether they think they have the DNA or not!"
Jason Alba, CEO of JibberJobber.com, Speaker, Author

"We can learn valuable lessons from the experience of others. Sean's collection of knowledge in developing and running successful businesses provide a powerful tool for new and experienced business owners. I encourage you to read this book and apply the lessons you learn."
Thomas Jenkins, Owner, Viking Appraisal Services

"'DNA of the Young Entrepreneur' is very straightforward and explains simply and clearly the step-by-step processes for building and managing a successful company. What strikes us about Sean and reading DNA is this: it is one thing to be so completely successful as an entrepreneur at such a young age, but to then have the ability and talent to write the HOWs and WHYs so straightforwardly make this book a must read."
Dennis and Kathleen Erba, Owners/Brokers, Coldwell Banker Coast Properties

Author

- Sean McCauley
  smccauley@mccauleyinv.com

Publisher

- Mitchell Levy
  http://happyabout.info

Editing & Layout

- Teclarity
  http://teclarity.com

Cover Design

- Mark Elias
  markselias@gmail.com

Dedication

To Maria, Marissa, Mallory, and Michaela, my devoted daughters and wife. Thank you for your support and patience.

Acknowledgments

I want to express my thanks to all the people in my life who have made me what I am. My wife, first of all, who has been by my side giving me the encouragement, advice, and (let's face it) rebukes that have kept me focused and on track. To all the people close to me who impact my life daily. Thanks to my publisher, Mitchell Levy, for giving the book the chance to see the light of day. Thanks to Don Huntington, without whom the book would not have been written. I give special thanks to my Lord and Master, Jesus Christ, who in good times and bad has blessed me throughout the years of my life.

A Message from Happy About®

Thank you for your purchase of this Happy About book. It is available online at http://happyabout.info/dna.php or at other online and physical bookstores.

- Please contact us for quantity discounts at sales@happyabout.info
- If you want to be informed by email of upcoming Happy About® books, please email bookupdate@happyabout.info

Happy About is interested in you if you are an author who would like to submit a non-fiction book proposal or a corporation that would like to have a book written for you. Please contact us by email editorial@happyabout.info or phone (1-408-257-3000).

Other Happy About books available include:

- Confessions of a Resilient Entrepreneur: http://happyabout.info/confessions-entrepreneur.php
- They Made It!: http://happyabout.info/theymadeit.php
- The Successful Introvert: http://happyabout.info/thesuccessfulintrovert.php
- Wealthy U: http://happyabout.info/wealthyu.php
- Memoirs of the Money Lady: http://happyabout.info/memoirs-money-lady.php
- 42 Rules™ of Cold Calling Executives: http://happyabout.info/42rules/coldcallingexecutives.php
- Marketing Campaign Development: http://happyabout.info/marketingcampaigndevelopment.php
- Happy About CEO Excellence: http://happyabout.info/ceo-excellence.php
- 42 Rules™ for Sensible Investing: http://happyabout.info/42rules/sensible-investing.php
- Happy About LinkedIn for Recruiting: http://happyabout.info/linkedin4recruiting.php
- Collaboration 2.0: http://happyabout.info/collaboration2.0.php
- Happy About Customer Service?: http://happyabout.info/customerservice.php
- Blitz the Ladder: http://happyabout.info/blitz.php

Contents

Introduction

This is a book for young adults who have the drive, attitude, and intelligence required for business success, but who lack an understanding of what success requires and are confused about how to get started.

I'm writing this book especially for young entrepreneurs who have the urge to get out of the run-of-the-mill daily grind of working for The Man and lift themselves to the next level where they can be masters of their own fate and perhaps accrue more wealth than would be possible in any 9-to-5 job.

The book is also for the entrepreneur who is stuck in a rut and looking for assistance in getting themselves to the next level of success.

Some people have the motivation, intelligence, and energy to do well in business, but don't have a path to follow to success.

I'll help motivate you in discovering your own dream and will show you illustrations of the framework that will guide you to success, plus examples of the sort of attitude and commitment required to enable you to get there.

If you want to learn how to get into business for yourself or to succeed in the business you already have, this is the book for you. I'm not giving you a manual for starting and running your business, but providing the lessons I learned and the principles I discovered that got me to where I am. I've learned the lessons and have identified the principles required to be successful and I'm glad to share them with you.

One of my life's goals is to share what I have done with other people and to assist them in achieving success of their own. So now I'm giving you the real deal—the information that will enable you to overcome and conquer and to figure out what it takes to make it in business today.

1 My Way to Wealth

The Triathlon endurance sport tests people's strength and will. Some people would consider swimming ten laps in a health club swimming pool to be a test of endurance, but Ironman competitors swim two-and-a-half miles, which is equivalent to 176 laps. Some people would consider a ten-mile bike ride a good day's exercise, but Ironman competitors ride 112 miles. Many people would have difficulty running two miles, but Ironman competitors run more than 26 miles. And they do all three grueling events back to back in a single day!

Engaging at a competitive level in a high-endurance sport requires not only supreme effort during times of actual competition, but even more importantly, such a sport calls for many hours, days, and months of intense and committed preparation for the demands that the actual competition will place upon the athlete's body. I spent nine months training for my first Ironman by swimming 3,000 yards every morning, and either running eight miles or biking 25–30 miles every afternoon.

If you speak to someone that has completed one of these races you will always hear them say that it is mostly a mental sport. In other words, if you are not mentally prepared for this venture you will never make it.

Competing in and completing an Ironman provides a fitting metaphor for my attitude towards life, in general, and towards conducting business, in particular. In all areas of my life I remain prepared, keep my eyes on the goal, and maintain constant forward progress. I endure the daily discipline and even punishment required for success. I'm willing to pay the price.

I grew up in what some might consider a disadvantaged childhood. I endured poverty and grinding challenges beyond anything most of my schoolmates endured. Early on, I learned that difficulties can either wear us down or build us up and learned to use problems as a basis for positive action—the more difficult the challenges become, the more opportunity they provide for learning and growth.

Helen Keller, who being both blind and deaf had a right to speak about such things, wrote the words,

> *Character is not built in ease and quiet. Only through experience of trial and suffering can the soul be strengthened, vision cleared, ambition inspired, and success achieved.*

The challenges of life have made me what I am today, and the best thing you can learn from me is to not be turned back by difficulties but to confront them—using each one as a basis for learning that will help you step into a better future than you would have discovered otherwise.

Don't be afraid of failures. A wise person once wrote, *Three failures denote uncommon strength. A weakling has not enough grit to fail thrice.* And Mickey Rooney said, *You always pass failure on your way to success.*

The secret is to find a place of emotional, social, financial, and spiritual balance. Otherwise you will experience failures from which you will not be able to recover.

We need an Ironman's attitude in facing all of life, including our business. We must regard challenges and difficulties with a smile on our face, passion in our heart, and steel in our soul. We prepare ourselves to endure the trials when they come because we believe that they will surely come.

In the following pages I'll describe for you the lessons I've learned from life and from the mistakes I've made. If you are wise you will let my hard-earned lessons protect you from making some of these mistakes yourself.

Here's a word of advice about getting the most benefit from the following pages: Don't imagine that simply reading this book will automatically make you successful. Don't read this as you would a novel or mystery. Take time to master the material and to apply it to your own life.

Read *Section 1 - My Way to Wealth* with careful understanding. Take notes, because in these pages I describe the idea of success, together with the principles, disciplines, and tasks that belong to effective entrepreneurship. These are important building blocks for laying a foundation of success for yourself that will change your life as you make them part of your thinking and understanding.

The power to dramatically transform the way you do business is the 39 principles that make up *Section 2 - The Angel's in the Details*. The description of each principle concludes with several action items, which are steps you can take to implement that particular principle in your life. These action items are real tasks that will unlock the power of each principle and put them to work for you.

Becoming successful in any business requires a lot of effort and commitment. It doesn't get any easier, however, than reading this book, absorbing the material presented, and then putting it into practice as you strive to develop your own successful business.

The benefits that you will reap from this book will be exactly equal to the amount of effort you put in to understanding and implementing the things that I am going to explain to you.

Expending the effort required to really absorb the following material and then incorporating the learning into your own life will become an important indicator that you really do have the right stuff that will enable you to become successful.

It's with much satisfaction that I've put these pages together for you!

Have fun with this stuff. Take your time and get this right.

1 Grasp the Idea of Success

Because of my own entrepreneurial successes a number of young, ambitious men and women have asked me the question of how to become successful. I might have won a Pulitzer Prize if I could have formulated an answer that would have given them a sure-fire path towards the future they dreamed of.

The problem is that success isn't simple enough to reduce to a formula or proverb. One of the many complexities is the issue of how to define success. If you limit success to simply making a lot of money, then what is required is for you to simply find the business opportunity that will enable you to accumulate wealth.

But once you became rich would you, in fact, then really be successful? We've known abject failures who have had millions and even billions of dollars in the bank but who nevertheless led shattered existences due to their inability to maintain balance in their lives.

In my eyes such people are not smart business-men or businesswomen no matter how much money they have made. They achieved what they wished for but failed to get what they needed.

Wealth and success are two different things. After Elvis Presley had achieved fame and wealth, a reporter asked him, "Have you everything you want now?" Elvis replied, "No, I'll tell you one thing. I sometimes get lonely as hell."

The fact is that the two common accouterments of success mentioned in the quote—wealth and fame—can never by themselves provide the content of success.

Dale Carnegie said that you never achieve real success unless you like what you are doing. One definition of success that appeals to me is to find the thing in life that you like doing most of all—the gift you have been given that sets you apart from others—and then figuring out how to make money at that.

A passenger plane experienced some electronic failure and the captain made the announcement, *The bad news is that we've lost our navigation system and have no idea where we are. The good news is that we've picked up the jet stream and are going faster than this plane has ever gone before.*

Not knowing where you are heading makes it difficult to arrive at your destination no matter how fast you go!

You create power for living and energy for business when you figure out where you want to go and then start going in that direction. But along the way you have to live a life that is balanced and fulfilled.

I imagine that at one time Elvis would have said that singing is the thing that he liked doing most of all. If he had just focused his life on giving to the world his gift of music, he would have been successful by his own definition. But somewhere he lost sight of the gift and turned aside to whatever lesser things filled his life, whether money, sex, drugs, alcohol, material possessions...he didn't stay grounded. His life got off-balance. He didn't maintain his focus upon the goal that he wanted to achieve in life.

Figuring out what success would mean to you—how much it would cost, how much you really want it—is the first step.

Step two is to begin to transform yourself into a person of success. Success is an inside-out job. You have to improve yourself before you try to improve your circumstances.

If you want to start your own business and build some wealth then prepare yourself for possibly the hardest thing you're going to do in your life. We're working out the truth of the proverb, *Lazy hands make a man poor, but diligent hands bring wealth.* Or, as Thomas Edison put it, *Opportunity is missed by most people because it comes dressed in overalls, and it looks like work.*

A lot of people shouldn't attempt to become wealthy because the road to riches is a difficult one and takes a lot more work than most people are willing to commit to. Looking back on many of my ventures, the journeys to my goals, not the accomplishments, were the most rewarding.

Robert Frost said that by working faithfully eight hours a day, a person may eventually get to be a boss and work 12 hours a day. But even that's optimistic. I worked a lot of 12-hour days before I ever owned my own company. I became my own boss because I was willing to work 12 hours a day for someone else.

People who don't want to make that effort should find contentment with a 9-to-5 kind of life and with the condominium-level existence that goes along with that.

The only group of us who will succeed are those who bring to the table the gifts, grit, and gumption to make a business work.

But the great fact is that hard work is not only the key to wealth, but also provides a zest for life—a delight in living—that those of us with the true entrepreneurial spirit can find no place else. The poet and greeting card entrepreneur, Susan Polis Schutz, wrote:

> When you have a goal in life that takes a lot of energy, that requires a lot of work, that incurs a great deal of interest, and that is a challenge to you, you will always look forward to waking up to see what the new day will bring.

If you'll stay with me for the next several chapters, I'll show you how to channel that kind of attitude into wealth.

Chapter

2 Carry Out Five Tasks for Success

Successful people are distinguished from those who fail on the basis of whether or not they've done the things that contribute to success. So we'll begin with an overview of the specific actions involved in every successful business venture.

Many businesses flounder and fail almost before they get started because the ill-equipped would-be entrepreneur has not identified the tasks that will make the business succeed. Norman Vincent Peale gave a prescription for success when he wrote,

> *Formulate and stamp indelibly on your mind a mental picture of yourself as succeeding. Hold this picture tenaciously. Never permit it to fade. Your mind will seek to develop the picture.... Do not build up obstacles in your imagination.*

In other words, know where you are going; identify exactly what you need to do in order to get there.

I've compiled and assembled the multitude of finely granulated tasks that provide for success into a polished list of five items. In any business—from selling lemonade to manufacturing long-range jet air-craft—there are five primary things you need to do to be successful.

My own success has been predicated upon my carrying out the following five important tasks:

Task #1 - Create Excitement

Emerson spoke the truth when he observed that nothing great was ever achieved without enthusiasm. He wrote, *The world belongs to the energetic.* A sense of eagerness and excitement are fundamental requirements for success in every important enterprise. I would never get out of bed in the morning before the sun came up to swim 3,000 yards in preparing for the Ironman if I didn't have a sense of excitement about being in the game. I carry that enthusiasm to all aspects of my life.

As the world continues to grow more complicated it becomes increasingly more difficult to be successful without having a lot of passion. Some business owners are able to be successful with a business-as-usual approach, but their companies will never reach their full potential. All parts of life, and especially everything in business, will thrive best with an air of animation. It is up to me, as an entrepreneur, to maintain passion for the project and to instill this in my people.

The excitement has to be centered upon things that are actually happening. I keep in front of each employee the answer to the question, *What is in this for me?* I work to maintain the *esprit de corps* that will motivate everyone to work as a unit, pulling together in the same direction because of the conviction that each will benefit from the success that we create together.

The goal is to make the work so exciting and rewarding that people won't be tempted to play solitaire during work time, or spend hours buying and selling on eBay, or checking the help-wanted section of the newspaper.

Remember that you are under a microscope. Your employees will imitate your actions, behaviors, and attitudes. You are the one setting the tone for everyone in the company. As you go, so will your entire business. Therefore, make sure you are always going in the right direction—leading others to success as they follow in the path that you, by your example, are setting for them.

How you behave when you arrive to the office in the morning will help set the emotional environment for the day. There have been occasions when business challenges have put me through the wringer. People I've worked with understood the terrible situations that I was going through, at times, with serious cash-flow issues, accidents, illnesses...they don't need to be reminded of the stress, that's your responsibility as a leader; don't take it out on your team.

Tough times give leaders opportunities to shine. There is absolutely no place in any business for leaders to conduct pity parties or bitch sessions. A sullen attitude or a gloomy countenance will bring down the emotional climate of the whole team. We need to be strong, confident—usually full of good cheer but always running over with confidence.

If your employees know that you have problems but you come through the door exuding an air of encouragement and hope, you will lift the workplace atmosphere and morale.

People are like tea bags. Hot water brings out the essence of their nature. You can get a team to follow you anywhere if you show them grace under pressure. My employees have developed fierce loyalty to me, in part because they have seen me handle problems that would have broken them.

A pastor once asked an acquaintance of mine how he was doing.

"Fine," the guy answered, "...under the circumstances."

"Well, what are you doing under the circumstances?" the pastor asked.

Someone pointed out that pain is inevitable but suffering is optional. We're all going to experience difficult circumstances but none of us have to be crushed by them—and for the sake of our business and for our example before the people working for us, we'd better not be *under* the circumstances, whatever they are.

Task #2 - Assemble a First-Rate Team

One of the important challenges in any of my businesses is to locate people with the appropriate levels of knowledge, experience, and intelligence to carry out the tasks assigned to them. The profoundly wise John Welch, instructed us to *get the right people on the bus*. Once you have them safely aboard, then it becomes equally important to get them in the right seat.

Don't run your business as a corporate animal. Understand that a big business and an entrepreneur-level project are two different creatures. Some of the things that run the corporate world are transferable to entrepreneurial enterprises—such as paying attention to the metrics of the company, setting up effective policies and procedures, and paying attention to HR issues. But these things aren't what we're about.

Middle and even upper-level managers in large corporations have the luxury of running an enterprise by rote process. When they try to break off to start their own business, they get into trouble by assuming that they can replicate the larger business's success simply by doing business *by the numbers*.

People who try to do this often fail because they do not take into account what I call the *Human Capital Asset*. In big companies things happen by policy and procedure, but in entrepreneurial-size companies they happen by people.

I spent several years working with a Fortune 250 company doing mostly Mergers and Acquisitions. This required me to look at small businesses and try to predict their success. I was very good at the job because the number one thing I looked for was Human Capital while continually seeking to answer the question, *What kind of employees will we be getting if we acquire this company?*

If there was no core of good people coming on board I would walk away from the deal even if the business model they were using was a good one. On the other hand, if the business plan was a little shaky but the people were great, I would be tempted to work with the situation. You can fix business operations but you can't fix people.

When I started my first company, I was totally aware of the importance of the Human Capital Asset and understood the principle: You need good people more than you need anything else.

If you are putting enough intelligence and heart into the effort, finding these human assets might not be as difficult as you might imagine. Most people may seem ill-equipped by attitude and training to excel in any job, but enthusiasm and energy will create vibrations that draw good people towards us. Or perhaps it's a condition of the moral universe that excellent opportunities attract excellent people.

One thing we modern entrepreneurs have going for us at this point is that people who have labored to become superior at some line of work are naturally looking for superior opportunities both to demonstrate and to profit from the abilities that they have developed. Such people gravitate towards opportunities to commit themselves to and grow with a company that they can see is worthy of their superior potential.

I search for the foundation qualities such as loyalty, intelligence, diligence, and commitment. Basic skills are less important because in a few days you can teach a bright, motivated person to perform data entry or drive a truck. But a computer specialist or professional teamster who lacks those foundation qualities won't be a superior worker after two or three years on the job.

It is as important that a team member be trustworthy as it is that they be capable. I will never waste unnecessary resources attempting to protect myself and my business from possible harm or loss caused by someone whom I am unable to trust. No deceitful or disloyal person will ever help me thrive in my business no matter what other traits they might possess.

A good team member also needs to have the important characteristic of being willing to learn and grow in a job. I was hiring a manager for a new area of one of my businesses. Two people wanted the position. One had been with me three years; another for eight years. We concluded that the one with lesser seniority was the better person for the position.

The senior person was upset at being passed over. "Why did you choose this guy? I've been here for eight years."

"No," I said, "You've been here one year eight times; he's actually been here for three years."

That might have been a little harsh, but it pointed out a characteristic of alertness and teachability that we entrepreneurs need to search for, latch onto and then honor when we find it.

Creating effective relationships with people demands that I, as an entrepreneur, be both tough and generous—as quick to eliminate under-performers, malingerers, and dishonest employees as I am to reward excellence and commitment.

You will never succeed in creating an abundantly successful business unless you learn how to find the right people and then move them into the right positions. Later on, in *Section 2*, we will spend time and learn one of the hardest things a young entrepreneur must master, how to find and choose these people.

Task #3 - Lead by Follow-Up

Successful team building and business growth are accomplished by cooperative efforts on the part of everyone involved. My function as owner and top executive is not to rule but to serve. I don't expect people to try to make me look good or help me to feel good about myself. Just the opposite! I work hard to make them look good and to feel good about themselves, especially about the job they are doing for the company.

Since I am admittedly not the smartest or most capable person in any of my companies, what I do is to manage my employees in order to keep them operating at peak efficiency and effectiveness. I do everything I can to reward and to retain top performers. I share profits with them and praise them for good work. Every one of them is important to my success.

I don't want them to work because they fear getting fired if they screw up; I want to motivate them by sharing with them my vision of what the company is trying to do and what success can mean for us all.

I maintain a hands-on attitude towards my businesses. I'm a firm believer in the principle that you should never ask others to do something that you wouldn't do yourself. I'm not afraid to get my hands dirty. I seldom wear a suit. I rub shoulders with my people and would do anything to help get the job done. I care about them and they know it. My own attitude reinforces their healthy sense of self-worth, on one hand, and their commitment to the business, on the other.

The most important people on my org charts are the customers and my employees interfacing with them in the field. That's where the real business is taking place. Everything else in the company, including my own efforts, should focus upon maximizing most effectively the people operating at that level.

In my early years as a businessman, I got the idea of turning my org charts upside down in order to put the people in the field and the customers at the top with management at the lower levels and me at the bottom. I continue to operate my businesses by this structure.

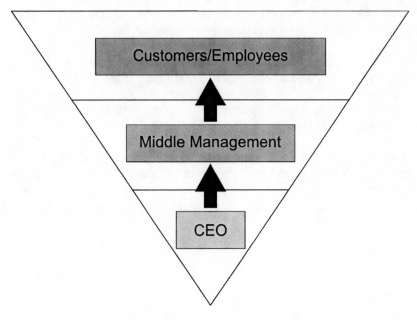

Figure 1: Inverted Org Chart

The bottom line in my businesses are strengthened as I take care of my people and my people take care of my customers. That's worked for me in every business I have. The service business I developed, for example, grew so quickly because I expended a lot of resources in cultivating the people who work for me. I invested time by inspiring them and by training them to their full potential.

Every meeting I tell people, *I'm here to serve you.* It's my attitude. I tell all my managers, *We are here to serve people; then they will take care of the business.*

Task #4 - Communicate the Business Plan to Everyone

My success in any business depends directly upon my successfully communicating to stakeholders in the company the vision and information that they need to perform at the top of their game. I instill in my team members a clear vision of where they are going. Each employee, from the top-level manager to the lowest person in the trenches, must clearly understand where our business is in the marketplace, what we do, and where we are going.

Not only is it my responsibility to ensure that our corporate values are in place, but I have to make sure that people working for me are actually operating in accordance with them.

Businesses waste millions of dollars employing workers who don't really understand what kind of business they are in and so fail to do things that bring profits to the bottom line. If employees are wasting time and goofing off, then their actions jeopardize business and endanger their job security. Therefore, it's supremely important to me to ensure that my managers are successfully communicating to our employees what we are trying to accomplish.

Happy customers are the source of profits, a fact that requires all of us to successfully convey our vision and mission statement to the people we're serving. Customer service is more than half the business. If my employees tell customers they will show up between 1:00 and 3:00 in the afternoon and don't get there until after dark, I'm losing business even if I'm making money on that particular job.

People working for me all understand that we ultimately make money by satisfying customers and not by simply collecting on invoices. If customers or clients are disappointed by the quality of our products or services, then we've failed even if we collect a payment from them.

I expect full-hearted cooperation from each of my employees; we're all in this together to make the company successful, or my employees can't stay in the game with me.

I heard the story of the CEO of an airline who, without announcement or fanfare, walked up to one of the customer service desks belonging to his airline. Nobody was behind the desk except for a man who was reading a magazine.

Suddenly the phone began to ring.

After several rings the CEO asked the loafer, "Aren't you going to answer that?"

"No," the man replied. "That's not my job."

So the CEO walked around the desk, answered the phone, and did what he could to help the person who had been calling.

After hanging up the loafer looked at the CEO in surprise.

"Do you work here?" the man asked.

"Yes," the CEO replied. "But you don't anymore."

I applaud the CEO's attitude of insisting that employees serve the business without erecting barriers around what they will and will not do.

However, my goal is to communicate the business plan, together with the personal implications of the plan, to everyone in the company, and to make sure that everyone is, in fact, on board with the business. That they are provided with the opportunity to join in as a welcome team member to improve their own lot as they work for the enrichment of the company. This is enormously more effective than holding the threat of job termination over them should they fail to show the right spirit.

It is up to us to find out whether or not employees have bought into the program at a heart-felt level. Then, let them decide whether they are willing to get into the game or resign. They can always look for some sinecure job that doesn't require that kind of loyalty and effort that we are looking for. After all, those kinds of jobs are all over. Working to the very lowest level of your energy is what many government positions in post offices, Departments of Motor Vehicles, and the myriad regulatory agencies are all about.

These kinds of jobs are also available in most union shops. Every union contract has at its heart the goal of protecting people, like the loafer behind the airline desk, from having to do things like answer telephones if it isn't in their contract.

But we entrepreneurs can't work like that or have people like that working for us. And who would want to work like that? There are people who are willing to engage in their jobs with all their hearts. We just have to find them. They are all over the place and anxious to work for people like us.

Find them. Communicate the business plan to them. Get them excited. If you treat them right they'll work their heart out for you.

Task #5 - Delegate Work

Next to your time people are the most valuable resource in almost any business venture. Unless you are doing some small work-from-home business you will not be able to do everything yourself. The wisdom to make the right decisions about what tasks and responsibilities to retain personally, and which ones you need to hand off to someone else, is one of the most critical parts of managing any business.

My most important task is to stay on top of things and to understand what is actually happening at all levels of each of my companies. If I don't know my business better than anyone else knows it, the business will never dominate its particular niche.

My knowledge then permits me to effectively place the right people into the right positions and ultimately do the right things. Almost nothing is more important than assigning to people with the required skills, talents, and attitudes appropriate tasks together with the correct authority to act and make decisions.

The challenge for me is to avoid the twin errors of not providing sufficient supervision on one hand and inappropriately micromanaging employees' tasks on the other. Accountability and trust are the two keys for finding the right balance. Through accountability, goals are set so that subsequent progress can be measured and reported. Appropriate acknowledgement is made for meeting and exceeding goals, and corrective actions or revisions are made when goals are not met. When accountability processes are conducted in an atmosphere of trust, a healthy situation is created that eliminates the need for endless reports verifying and validating the process.

Sometimes you can teach a person trust by actually trusting him. Henry L. Stimson once said, *The chief lesson I have learned in a long life is that the only way to make a man trustworthy is to trust him; and the surest way to make him untrustworthy is to distrust him and show your distrust.*

Accountability and trust are the means whereby I get past the principle, *If you want a job done right then do it yourself.* I can't emphasize enough how important it is for me to realize that I usually can't do individual tasks belonging to my businesses as well as the specialists I've hired can. I provide them with sufficient training and incentives so they really grow into their job—becoming much better than I am and, in some cases, becoming far better than I could possibly be.

I think an unfortunate dumbing-down takes place in some businesses because entrepreneurs are threatened by the presence of anyone smarter than themselves. But my attitude is just the opposite because I'm encouraged when I've hired someone brighter or more talented than myself.

How bright is it for me to seek to get the best people possible to work for me? How dim would I have to be to try to maintain my own level of intelligence as the highest that I'll permit in my company?

Don't be afraid to praise. Many supervisors have mistakenly believed that if you praise people for excellent performance you run the risk that they will take advantage of the situation by believing that if the boss was pleased then perhaps they worked harder than was necessary. Just the opposite is actually true. A slap on the back or a *Good job!* will only cause good workers to increase their efforts. Actual research has demonstrated that most of us prefer a sincere commendation for a job well done to receiving a bonus.

When you need to correct or rebuke an employee, you can soften the effect and save the person's pride by adding a praise at the end of the transaction. If you tell someone, *You are one of our top performers when you are here, but you have too many absences,* the effect is altogether different than if you say, *You have too many absences even though, when you are here, you are one of our best performers.*

I say this because appropriate feedback is a key component to delegation. Some people delegate responsibility but then never revisit that decision. A great leader, on the other hand, will follow up and praise a project or job duty well done by a particular team member. Or, when appropriate, give the constructive criticism to employees in order to help them improve.

3 Get in the Habit of Success

I'm always trying to find how to better myself year after year. Fifteen years ago I had the goal of running three days a week. Now I train twice a day. That's progress you can see and measure!

Aristotle said, *We are what we repeatedly do*, and then added an obvious deduction, *Excellence, then, is not an act but a habit*. My goals are aimed at creating habits that will develop me. In fact, I judge goals against the single criterion of habits. An inferior goal is one that leads only to some accomplishment. It is static, lifeless, and ultimately unproductive beyond a single outcome.

For example, I might set a goal to buy a new car. That's not a good goal because it is too easy, with a puny short-term payoff and no residual change in my character or in the quality of my life.

Or I might set as a goal to become wealthy. This is an insufficient goal for the opposite reason as the first one: it is ill-defined. It will never happen because the goal doesn't contain in itself even the hint of any activities or tasks that will lead to an accomplishment.

A productive goal, on the other hand, is one that leads to the development of some good habit. The habit, in turn, leads to an accomplishment. For example, I might decide to meditate and read the Bible a half hour each morning or I might spend a half hour reading from a volume of the World's Greatest Literature set. After meeting this goal for a month or so it would have become a habit. After a year it would be difficult not to spend this time in meditation and reading.

Accomplishing the goal would change me. A half hour a day would mean that in a year I would have spent a period of time totaling more than a week in the company of people like Moses or the Apostle Paul—or with such people as Plato and Shakespeare. I would be changed by the experience; the habit would make me a better man.

Or I might decide to save 10 percent of my income. After a year, or so, it would become an ingrained habit and I wouldn't even have to think about it any more. My account would simply have a steadily increasing flow of cash that I could use for investments, vacation, or whatever.

Or I might decide to run ten miles a week. In a year I will have run a distance of 520 miles, which is equal to running from San Francisco to Las Vegas, NV. The habit of running would have been solidly planted in my mind and schedule. My blood pressure would have decreased, my core would be strengthened, my breathing capacity would be increased, my weight reduced or maintained at an appropriate level....

In these three examples, the goal has changed me—improved me and made me a better and more productive person. The goal creates a dynamic that extends beyond a single accomplishment. By creating habit the goal develops an energy that will develop my life in positive ways far into the foreseeable future.

We all live by our habits so that the only way to improve your life is to improve your habits. And that isn't an easy task. *Habit is habit*, Mark Twain rightly observed, *and not to be flung out of the window by any man, but coaxed downstairs a step at a time.*

When you set goals for yourself, ask yourself the question, *Will this goal create a positive habit for me in my life?* If the answer is *No!* then don't make this a goal.

I revise my list of goals before January each year. Revising the goals takes weeks of intensive commitment and soul searching. You can't just set habit-changing goals in an afternoon.

We've all met people who are prone to make the same mistake over and over again—to compulsively repeat acts that bring their lives down—never learning from their mistakes and eventually becoming wretched human beings. They develop habits of failure. Someone said that, *A bad habit is the worst boss anyone can have.* The fact is that when you have a bad habit, you really are serving a terrible master.

We build for success on discipline. We achieve success in each area of our lives by developing habits for success in those areas.

There is no shortcut. *Whatever a man sows, that shall he also reap,* runs an old and true proverb. The disciplines of my life, outlined above, are simply tangible definitions of what sowing for my success actually looks like.

4 Put into Place Disciplines for Success

Even though success requires a lot of time and effort on the job, the job itself is only one part of a successful life. I've discovered that a balanced, truly fulfilling life involves setting goals around what I call the five *F's*. These include Family, Finances, Fellowship, Faith, and Fitness.

I maintain a well-rounded life and keep on track on a daily basis by setting and working on goals according to these five important sets of habitual behaviors. The five F's are the core structure around which I build my life; they form the content of my success. To the extent that I'm doing well in each of these areas is the precise extent to which I count myself to be successful.

There's nothing vague about the evaluation of my success as measured against these five indicators because every year I create five measurable goals for each of the areas and then organize my activities for each year, month, week, and even day around the goals associated with each of the categories.

Someone said that a wise decision is the one that later you are glad you made. These goals are designed to help me make wise decisions that will push me towards my objectives in each of these areas and will make me pleased—even delighted—by each decision I make to push forward with each of them.

The F's are five spokes in the wheel of my life; the integrity of the whole structure would be compromised by weakness in any one of them.

Discipline #1 - Build Faith

Life is meaningless unless I can see how my life fits into a larger picture than can be framed by the boundaries of my businesses and my daily activities. Faith is the quality that equips me to receive the good things in the universe—the resources of grace that are always around us and always available for our taking.

Faith fits me into relationship with my Maker. The Bible says that without faith it is impossible to please God and then adds two obvious explanations: we must not only believe in His existence, but believe that He rewards our search for Him.

Faith is something I practice and not just something I think about. Faith is not something I debate about. Someone said that the heart has its reasons of which the reason knows nothing. So what would there be to argue about? I can *take hold of tomorrow with the handles of our faith* as a wise person said. Otherwise, how could I take hold of it? What significance could the future hold for me? Fortune and reputation would be ashes.

My faith is centered upon a personal relationship with Jesus Christ. He has become my True North providing the unchanging standard on which I can base my decisions.

I try to conduct myself according to a principle of conduct found in the Bible:

> *...in your hearts set apart Christ as Lord. Always be prepared to give an answer to everyone who asks you to give the reason for the hope that you have. But do this with gentleness and respect...*

In my opinion, such faith is founded upon sure facts concerning the nature of the universe, but it seems to me that practicing such a belief exerts a positive influence upon a person's life irrespective of the extent to which actual metaphysical realities are in accord with the tenants of a person's belief system. Research has consistently shown that Protestants, Catholics, Jews, and members of other religions are far more likely than are secular people to say they are happy.

Simply asserting that the world has meaning and purpose, and that a benevolent Power is providing good things for people who are willing to receive them, provides a positive basis for living and acting that is lost to people who believe the universe to be the result of random chance. An example of a faith-related goal for some might be reading their Bible for ten minutes a day. For others it may be to spend time in prayer each morning before they start their day. Whatever your faith goal is, the important thing is to make it something practical for you and then stick with it.

The positive effects of prayer, for example, have been demonstrated by scientific studies. Even more than that, a number of studies have suggested the effect prayer can exert upon reducing physical stress. A research project by Centra State Hospital discovered the psychological benefits of prayer to *reduce stress and anxiety, promote a more positive outlook, and strengthen the will to live.*

The challenge is always to bring the choices, actions, and attitudes of my life into alignment with my faith. The activist Catholic nun, Sister Helen Prejean, said, *I watch what I do to see what I really believe.* This reminds me of the old line, *What you are speaks so loud that the world can't hear what you say....*

It isn't *the world* that I'm mostly concerned about—it's that guy in the mirror whom I need to satisfy. If I can't be right for him, I can't be right for anyone. If my life is not in line with my beliefs, the cure is never to fix the beliefs.

The great Danish theologian, Søren Kierkegaard, called faith a *leap in the dark* and to some extent so it is. We leap into the abyss of some obviously correct action confident that *underneath are the everlasting arms* but we willingly make the jump even if it should turn out the arms aren't there. We do a lot of things just because they are the right things to do.

I've discovered the powerful principle that the best way to keep some things is to give them away. An effective route to personal development lies through deliberately teaching and encouraging others to share the beliefs and the attitudes that I want to develop in myself.

Faith plays a distinct role in my business success. I work because I believe that the daily activities of my life are merely extensions into the visible world of underlying realities that give my life substance, content, and significance.

Discipline #2 - Create Fellowship

I don't live in this world as a small island. The people who surround me assist me in maintaining and expanding my social and spiritual health. They give me opportunity to practice the characteristics of patience, kindness, love, and charity. Fellowship brings me into contact with people whom I can bless and who can bless my life. The Internet's Real Live Preacher correctly observed:

> *There isn't much better in this life than finding a way to spend a few hours in conversation with people you respect and love. You have to carve this time out of your life because you aren't really living without it.*

Fellowship is important because it provides an outlet to expand my life, starting with one-on-one relationships, which keep me grounded and helps me to understand the problems and issues of the people around me—the things they struggle with—while in turn, help me with mine.

An important part of success is sharing the success with other people. Not by writing checks into their bank accounts, but by helping them understand and imitate in their own lives the qualities that have made me successful in mine.

We take good things from the hand of God and from the guidance and example of other people, and then we pass them on to others. I'm paying forward to others from the reservoir of good things that are constantly coming to me. And I'm doing this deliberately. One of my Fellowship goals is to encourage one new person every month to become involved in a healthy lifestyle, and at least once a month to anonymously sponsor someone's attendance at some helpful seminar, workshop, or event that they could not otherwise afford.

I also have a Fellowship goal of inviting someone I would not usually spend time with to join in one of my activities, and this year to lead a climb up Yosemite's Half Dome with a small group that has never before done this.

I'm a believer in the old AT&T ad that we should *Reach out and touch someone* so at least once a month I have a Fellowship goal of renewing acquaintance with someone from my past. An idea that you could put into practice for one of your fellowship goals could be inviting someone you know to an event or social you go to that you normally would not think to take someone new with you to. You will be amazed at how much this will bless you as well as the person you invite. Another idea is to make it a goal to contact at least one friend or relative each month whom you have not spoken to for some time.

Fellowship plays a distinct role in my business success. The ability to meld my life with the lives of other people occasionally leads to a good business contact, of course, but more importantly, I learn lessons about being with other people that inevitably assist me in connecting with employees, clients, customers, and vendors.

Discipline #3 - Structure Finances

Money is no end in itself but provides for the blessings that we have in such things as our lovely home and the food we put on the table. Finances also help fund the expansion of our businesses. Not least of all, finances provide the means by which we can bless others less fortunate than ourselves and contribute to community development efforts. I'm moving from prosperity towards abundant prosperity one step at a time, demonstrating the principle from an old proverb that *Steady plodding brings prosperity.*

My goals in this area are straightforward and essentially self-explana-tory. As a guard against wastefulness and self-indulgence I've set as a Finance goal not to spend more than $1,000 on any item that will do nothing other than give me pleasure. I could spend $8,000 on a HD plasma display, for example, but the $7,000 that I refuse to spend on this could be invested, donated, or used in any number of better ways.

Other Finance goals include maxing out my 401k this year, reinvesting all passive income, and purchasing three new commercial investment properties.

In my personal finances I follow Thomas Jefferson's advice, *Never spend your money before you have it.* My actual policy is never to borrow money except for investing in products, services, or properties that will earn money.

Setting and meeting financial goals play the most obvious role in my business success. Many companies crash and burn for no other reason than that the owners and manager were unable to control costs and manage financial resources. I'm good at fiscal responsibility and, thanks to my Structure Finances goal, I get better every year. Some ideas on finance goals could be that you take 10% of your income and put it into a savings or an investment plan each month. Another direction you can go is to find an area that you may be spending more than you realized or are comfortable with. Set an amount that you would like to be the maximum amount that you would spend in this area each month and make it your goal to not go over that amount each month.

Discipline #4 - Practice Fitness

Good health provides a context in which the rest of my life can thrive. People who are feeling listless and enervated can never perform at the peak of their game. The time I spend on fitness activities is returned many times over in more effective thinking and working. Also, eating healthy and remaining in good physical condition are the best ways to maximize my chances of being around to enjoy my success, and to get to know my great-grandchildren.

Fitness can also have a spiritual quality. Many religions teach that the body is the dwelling place of God. The Bible, for example, asks the rhetorical question, *Do you not know that your body is a temple of the Holy Spirit?* My answer to that question is an unqualified *Yes!* I'm fulfilling the command at the end of the verse I quoted from above to, *...honor God with your body.* My exercise is joyful compliance with the command because when I'm out running I can empathize with Eric Liddell's comment, made famous in the movie Chariots of Fire, *I believe God made me for a purpose, but he also made me fast. And when I run I feel His pleasure.*

My five goals in the area of Fitness include one negative goal—that I will consume no processed food or soda. A health writer, Nancy Deville, wrote a book *Death by Supermarket*, subtitled *The Fattening, Dumbing Down, and Poisoning of America.* The title says it all! Some food products are being sold that are less nutritious than the packing material they come in. The cardboard wouldn't do you damage if you were to eat it, unlike some of the contents.

Being physically fit plays a role in my business success by making me more mentally alert and by giving me stamina to get through the sometimes long and stressful periods of work. I'm bright-eyed and ready for action even in the afternoon. I seldom get ill, and even when I am, I recover at a sometimes astonishing rate. In the area of setting your fitness goals, you want to be practical. Many set their goals too high and in return are setting themselves up for failure. If you are a person who currently does not have a workout plan at all, then you may want to start with a goal of walking for one hour a day, four days a week. If you are already one who currently works out but would like to improve, then you can choose to work with a trainer or just start working out with an accountability fitness partner. This will help you to stay motivated.

Discipline #5 - Focus on Family

My family is the center of my life—they provide the reason for working hard and a stable base for the rest of my life. My wife and daughters are the most important people in my life. Someone wrote, *If we die tomorrow, the company that we are working for could easily replace us in a matter of hours. But the family & friends we leave behind will feel the loss for the rest of their lives.*

That works both ways. If one of my companies failed, I would just pick up the pieces and go to the next thing. But the loss of one of my family members would create a loss that nothing but a heavenly reunion would ever be able to restore.

My wife and daughters create a home life for me and provide a context in which the other pieces of my life actually fit together. The five of us are a critical mass. We find identity and stability in our association with each other. Together we put down roots deep into the social fabric of the world.

My devotion to my family drives me towards moral purity. I'm following the lead of the psalmist who wrote, *I will lead a life of integrity in my own home. I will refuse to look at anything vile and vulgar.* The passage makes the psalmist sound like he predicted Internet porn and echoing his determination in my own life provides a safeguard against going to websites, for example, that would make me ashamed before my wife and daughters if they knew what I was doing.

Paul Tournier made the wise observation that *Nothing makes us so lonely as our secrets.* Internet pornography isn't the worst thing in the world, but it creates a secret life for some men that really does serve to isolate them from their families in ways that they can't begin to understand.

Especially when these guys maintain a façade of moral honor to cover the sexual pandering that goes on in front of their computer screens does the harsh denial of their integrity rip at their lives. Anybody with an open and unconcealed affection for illicit sex is preferable to those people who try to pretend a virtue that they don't posses.

The healthiest family relationships are founded upon sexual faithfulness—in both deed and thought—to the spouse, as exhibited before the children. Someone said that the best thing a father can do for his children is to remain in love with their mother.

My Family goals mitigate the possibility of my engaging in secret and shameful behaviors because they focus my attention upon my family and upon meeting their needs. One of the needs they have is for me to be pure in my love for their mother.

Specific Family goals could include surprising the family with a day-trip that they weren't expecting, participating on a school field trip, scheduling a family vacation, occasionally surprising your spouse with an unexpected date without the kids, and/or going on a date with a different child of yours each month.

You will find that as you go from year to year setting these goals for yourself that they will change quite a bit from year to year. I find that my goals drive me forward. I do my best to work on them everyday.

I keep a copy of my goals prominently displayed in each of my offices. I monitor my progress. To not attain each of these goals would be to fall short in investing in my life those things that will make me successful. And I will do everything within my own power to not fail or come up short in any of them! The five areas are the parts of my life that create balance. I couldn't eliminate any piece without instantly creating instability.

The five goals themselves are non-negotiable and you shouldn't tamper with them. I encourage you to make a list. Spend time getting this right. And then spend time each day working on each goal.

Monitor your progress. Get an accountability partner who will encourage you to remain faithful. Don't ever stop. You will never be the same!

Below is an example of the sheet I use to fill out my goals at the start of each year.

Five F's of _____
(current year)

	Faith
1.	
2.	
3.	
4.	
5.	
	Family
1.	
2.	
3.	
4.	
5.	
	Fitness
1.	
2.	
3.	
4.	
5.	
	Fellowship
1.	
2.	
3.	
4.	
5.	
	Finances
1.	
2.	
3.	
4.	
5.	

2 The Angel's in the Details

The comic strip Dilbert amuses many people, because it light-heartedly mirrors their experiences in the corporate world. They recognize that, all too often, executives make decisions without a clear understanding of the ins and outs of the business.

Many companies are simply scraping by or failing because there are many parts of the business in which it appears that nobody is actually minding the store.

The Bible spoke truly when it wrote that the little foxes ruin the vines. Not usually the elephantine beasts of some disaster, but the little varmints of things left undone and duties left unattended gradually bring many business ventures to ruin.

Sir Arthur Conan Doyle, who was something of a specialist when it came to details, once remarked, *It has long been an axiom of mine that the little things are infinitely the most important.*

Someone said that *the Devil's in the Details*, and, in fact, paying insufficient attention to the collection of minutia concerning markets, vendors/suppliers, clients/customers, personnel, products, compliance with government regulations, bookkeeping tasks, quality control, payroll, etcetera that enable a business to thrive leads to the underperformance and failure of many promising ventures.

I'm actually switching the *devil's in the details* saying around. I consciously identify and attend to all the details of each of my businesses. I can say that *an angel is in the details*, because my companies end up at the top of their niche due to the fact that I'm attending to the business at a level of detail that many of my competitors will miss.

Below is a set of 39 principles encapsulating the details behind my business operations that made possible the transformation, bringing me from poverty to comparative wealth before the age of 40.

I've broken the principles down into four categories labeled: Becoming, Learning, Relating, and Doing. I've deliberately chosen active labels for these categories—using *becoming*, for example, rather than the more static label *being*, and *learning* rather than *knowing*.

The categories are arranged in a logical progression. The principles begin with *Chapter 5* - Principles About Becoming a Successful You. These are aimed at changing yourself. All the success you ever achieve will begin with you, because every positive accomplishment will be based upon the innate talents you bring to the challenges of life, plus the talents, attitudes, qualities, skills, and personal convictions that come to represent who you are.

You can maximize the personal qualities that will drive you to success if you discover your purpose for living, develop an attitude for success, learn to trust yourself, make up your mind to live ethically, remain focused and flexible as you live in the present, concentrate upon excellence, find the power of humility, and build upon failures.

If you concentrate upon these principles that will develop you as a human being, as a primary focus, then the development of your character will provide for the success of the principles to follow in the other categories.

The second category, *Chapter 6* - Principles About Learning to be Successful, guides you in learning those things that are required to successfully start a business and lead it to great success. These include preparation for success by learning about your business, identifying your market, identifying ways of providing products and service, learning about discipline, and about new ways of tackling the challenges of your business.

The third category, *Chapter 7* - Principles About Relating with People Successfully, will give you some foundational tools to guide you in creating positive and helpful relationships with employees, clients, customers, venders, etcetera, that lie at the heart of successful businesses and happy, satisfied entrepreneurs.

The chapter will describe the foundational roles that being good with partnerships, allocating people to the right jobs, giving people the power to succeed, using personality traits, and giving praise will play in ensuring success in your business.

Chapter 8 - Principles About Doing Things That Create Success is where the rubber meets the road. These principles talk about the actions you take to become successful—not accepting limitations, making decisions rationally, prioritizing, recognizing opportunities when they appear, leveraging changing conditions as potential sources of profit, identifying distribution channels for your products and services, moving your business to the point that it serves you rather than vice versa, and continually focusing on the basics that will ultimately ensure your success.

Note that, rather than being expressed as proverbs or maxims, each of the principles is worded in the form of a command. In other words, these are not simply matters for you to comprehend, they involve actions for you to take. In fact, each of the principles concludes with a short section usually beginning with words such as, *What am I going to do about...*that includes specific steps you can take to inculcate the principle in your own thinking as well as your actions.

5 Principles About Becoming a Successful *You*

One of the main qualities for all successful entre-preneurs is the ingrained and unshakable belief that they can succeed at whatever business they have decided to get into.

A sense of optimism, of course, is a valuable quality for anyone embarking on an entrepre-neurial adventure. But by itself, positive thinking isn't sufficient to guarantee success. The world is full of enthusiastic failures. A primary reason for failed businesses is failures going into business. The act of starting a business will not make people entrepreneurs any more than hanging out at McDonalds will make them a hamburger.

A true entrepreneur is a special person. Not everybody is equipped to run a business. Besides a proper attitude, any success that we enjoy as entrepreneurs will inevitably be based upon our talents, skills, qualities, and personal convictions.

A hopeful reality is that all of these can be culti-vated and dramatically improved except for the first one, *talents*. All of the others can be increased and improved. Provided you exert disciplined efforts in making the improvement. You can make these other areas strong enough to overcome a lack of talent.

For example, hockey star, Bobby Hull, was of slight build, and without natural physical talents but he showed ferocious hunger for success, developing mental and physical abilities that completely offset his limited physical gifts. Bobby Hull went on to become one of the greatest NHL players of all time.

A hugely successful motivational speaker, Rick Warren, described five measurements of growth: knowledge, perspective, conviction, skills, and character. Moving forward in these areas will constitute the Becoming that you need for success in life and business.

Read the following principles with care. Be sure you understand each of them—not just as mere head-knowledge, but incorporating each of them into your daily thinking and ensuring they become part of your decision-making process and affecting everything you do.

By mastering these Becoming principles, you will lay a solid base for excelling in the other principles and thus setting yourself up for the success that will come to you.

Principle #1 - Live for a Higher Purpose

The great preacher, William Cowper, once observed, *The only true happiness comes from squandering ourselves for a purpose.* Arnold Schwarzenegger spoke the truth when he said, *Being passionate about something is the key to success. But using that passion to help others is the key to happiness.*

The fact is that making money can never be your purpose in life, or else you will be a wretched poverty-stricken human being no matter how much wealth you accrue. Like Ebenezer Scrooge in Dickens' Christmas Carol, you will *derive no benefit* from the gold you hoard up for your own small intentions.

The famous American Journalist, Sydney J. Harris, once made a witty and sage observation, *Men make counterfeit money; in many more cases, money makes counterfeit men.* I heard of a man who once found a hundred-dollar bill lying by the side of the road; and he never saw the sun again.

In my experience many unfortunate people, some of them well off, are like that sad man. Heads down, oblivious to the sun, moon, stars, birds, and sunsets, they are searching for something that will never redeem the ultimate despair of their material-bound existence. They all have wings with which they could soar like eagles, but they are determined to walk upon the earth in their solitary and compulsive gloom.

Maurice Sendak, the great children's writer, hit the nail on the head when he observed, *There must be more to life than having everything.*

Success involves many things that are more important than simply accruing wealth. I'm here in this world for a reason. My life is *more than food and drink*, as the Bible says. Oprah once observed:

> *I've come to believe that each of us has a personal calling that's as unique as a fingerprint—and that the best way to succeed is to discover what you love and then find a way to offer it to others in the form of service, working hard.... The reward of a thing well done is to have done it.*

Those are wonderful words that I've noted in my own life.

Before you begin to make money learn what your purpose is. Discover that thing that gives you greatest satisfaction—the activity that you could do 12 hours a day for nothing—and then figure out how to make money at it.

In my own experience, my purpose in life that has led to relative wealth cannot be disassociated from my faith. It seems to me that faith has opened giant sluice gates of Heaven and poured down on me blessings of every kind. This has filled my heart with joy and my life with great purpose.

It's difficult for me to imagine coming to having a fine purpose in life unless that purpose is built upon the bedrock of faith. In an unguarded moment even the belligerent and brilliant atheist, Bertrand Russell, admitted that, *Unless you assume a God, the question of life's purpose is meaningless.*

Whatever your personal worldview may be, make it your purpose to do good in the world. Every genuine purpose has this component of serving others. The famous psychologist, Carl Jung, once observed, *As far as we can discern, the sole purpose of existence is to kindle a light in the darkness of being.*

And so as I'm working at my businesses with this higher purpose of serving God and humanity, I'm shining a light in the darkness that Jung spoke about—a radiance to light the way for others; a source of heat to warm their lives in this often-cold world.

Every good and noble purpose has at its heart an attitude of service for others. Marion Wright Edelman, a lifelong activist for the rights of children, wrote, *Service is the rent we pay for being. It is the very purpose of life, and not something you do in your spare time.*

A great by-product of working for some fine purpose that Heaven or the universe has led you to is that you become appropriately independent of others' opinions—neither demanding their approval nor crushed by their censure. John Bunyan, author of the incredible *Pilgrim's Progress*, made a telling observation about this: *If my life is fruitless, it doesn't matter who praises me, and if my life is fruitful, it doesn't matter who criticizes me.*

The fact is, no matter how marvelous your vision or how magnificent your accomplishments, some people will censure, scold, and perhaps even curse you. Look at what people said about President Bush, President Clinton, President Reagan…. William Thomas, an important politician, once denounced Abraham Lincoln as a Tyrant. Mobs crucified Jesus.

The higher your purpose the more certain will be your opposition. Albert Einstein correctly observed that, *Great spirits have always encountered violent opposition from mediocre minds....* He might also have said, *Great spirits have always ignored the opposition of mediocre minds.*

If you are sincere in your search for your higher purpose, you can live above both the curses and the adulation of the crowds. I'm following the advice of Kipling's great poem promising *the world and all that's in it* to people who follow his advice:

> *If you can bear to hear the truth you've spoken*
> *Twisted by knaves to make a trap for fools,*
> *Or watch the things you gave your life to broken,*
> *And stoop and build 'em up with worn-out tools....*

I'm living by faith, working for a high purpose, serving people, and earning a good income. Everything goes together.

What am I going to do about living life for a high purpose?

The following steps will direct you towards a purpose you can give yourself to:

1. Ask five of your friends what they think your best qualities are.

2. List on a sheet of paper 3–5 things that you did in the past six months that brought you the greatest satisfaction and made you feel the best about yourself.

3. List 3–5 business action steps you could take that would take into account the good qualities you've uncovered in step 1 and bring into play the things that brought you satisfaction in step 2.

4. Post the list of action steps in some place where you will see it every day; make this a living document; keep updating it; continue moving yourself in the direction of purpose-filled living and working. Make it a habit to live life on purpose.

Principle #2 - Develop an Indomitable Attitude

Mark Twain touched on an important point when he made the observation, *All you need is ignorance and confidence; then success is sure.* The comment is greatly exaggerated—ignorance will kill you in business as surely as a bad attitude will—but the underlying point is well taken. Confidence all by itself can achieve remarkable goals.

The behavioral psychologist, Denis Watley, observed, *Our limitations and success will be based, most often, on our own expectations for ourselves.* Then he gave the reason why this should be so: *What the mind dwells upon, the body acts upon.*

While growing up I worked much harder on the farm than I ever studied in the classroom. I got what they used to refer to as a *gentleman's C* because I had bigger fish to fry than any learning I could take away from a book and was eager to learn anything that caught my imagination and fit in with what seemed to me to be the important parts of life—things that had to do with working and developing skills that would help me become a man.

Teachers weren't able to capture and hold my attention because even as a youth I had the dominant and expressive personality of an entrepreneur. Most entrepreneurs are not particularly amiable or analytical. To paraphrase the lyrics of an old cowboy song, we won't do things to make you think we're right. I could never be an accountant. Forty hours a week of data analysis would drive me nuts.

Following graduation from high school I got a job doing pest control and the first day on the job I decided, *I'm going into business for myself. If this is what God wants for me then I'll do it.* I made up my mind that day that I was going to go all the way; I made the decision to open my own pest control company. That very day I started the journey towards wealth.

The business was doing well and when a competitor, Bill Todd, saw my determination he became a wonderful mentor. I developed such a thorough knowledge of the business that when the owner I worked for died two years later his two children, heirs of his estate, appointed me to run their father's company. Even though I was scarcely 20 years old, I was ready for business.

I was able to fight my way to success because I never doubted that I would succeed. The psychologist, Denis Watley, noted that, *A positive attitude is the best groundwork for positive accomplishments.* Helen Keller rightly noted, *No pessimist ever discovered the secrets of the stars, or sailed to an uncharted land, or opened a new heaven to the human spirit.*

Even more to the point, President Calvin Coolidge, who was known as a man of few words, issued a stirring challenge:

> *Press on: nothing in the world can take the place of perseverance. Talent will not; nothing is more common than unsuccessful men with talent. Genius will not; unrewarded genius is almost a proverb. Education will not; the world is full of educated derelicts. Persistence and determination alone are omnipotent.*

Diligence, which combines the *persistence* and *determination* that President Coolidge talked about, is the greatest gift a positive attitude can bestow. My success only came as I continued to work through a lot of challenges and difficult circumstance.

Woody Allen supposedly said that eighty percent of success is in showing up. I think I know what he means. Every morning I must once again carry out the activities that fulfill my life, keep my businesses strong, provide for the needs of my family, and create a positive impact upon the world around me.

The true basis of success lies not in the attempt to succeed simply for its own sake, but to learn to work to the limits of your abilities—to work with your whole heart to accomplish something fine in this world—not simply to succeed but rather to actually achieve something good.

The great movie star, Helen Hayes, said that her life was changed by a perceptive comment made by her mother concerning the difference between success and achievement:

Achievement is the knowledge that you have studied and worked hard and done the best that is in you. Success is being praised by others, and that's nice, too, but not as important or satisfying. Always aim for achievement and forget about success.

The difference between good businessmen and people with the capacity to become captains of industry lies in their adopting the mental attitude that will all but guarantee success.

How much do we want to be the best at our game? The answer to that question is what separates the minority who succeeds greatly and the great mass of entrepreneurs who wallow in mediocrity or failure. Our right attitudes are what motivate us to *sharpen the pencil* of our God-given talents and lead us to overcome any obstacles in our way.

The principle is summed up by one of the leading meditation teachers and spirituality writers, Sharon Salzberg, who wrote, *We learn and grow and are transformed not so much by what we do but by why and how we do it.*

With the right attitude you can achieve your goals; without it you are doomed to failure.

What am I going to do to implement the principle of developing an indomitable attitude?

The following steps will direct you towards developing the attitude you need:

1. Make a list of the 3–5 things that you are most fearful about in your business.
2. Under each item on the list put down at least two activities that would increase and build up your confidence in your ability to be successful.
3. Formulate and put into place plans to follow up on the activities identified in the previous step.
4. Find an accountability partner and share the list with them.

5. Review the list at regular interviews. Continue to attack the items with great vigor.

6. Revise the list, as things change in your life and business. Make it a habit to maintain a positive attitude.

Principle #3 - Trust Yourself

For every major business decision, be prepared to seek appropriate advice from lawyers, accountants, life coaches, and counselors whom you can trust. You especially should seek out successful professionals in your own line of business. Find out what they know that you could learn about becoming successful.

But, in the end you have to learn to trust yourself.

Find balance. I am in charge of my businesses and regard myself as the master of my own destiny, remembering that the success of my business will not be driven by the decisions that I allow other people to make for me. We all know that when we're standing on the end of the diving board of some big choice or crisis, we finally have to make the decision that we in our hearts believe to be the right one.

Most of the people you talk to are not wired like entrepreneurs; they will not see opportunities as clearly as you will. Some professionals in your field may even give you willfully wrong advice in order to reduce the threat that you represent as a competitor.

Learn to trust in your own business acumen above that of others. If you are an A-Type personality and are doing the due diligence that a new business requires, then you will quickly become the expert. Make it your goal, in fact, to become a leading expert in your field. Gather advice and wisdom from others but work towards the point at which you will be better equipped to make decisions than anybody else.

And then actually make the decisions. Too many businesses falter because of the inability of management to make decisions in a timely manner. When you have all the information that you need or are likely to get, don't dawdle. Learn to make decisions even if they turn out to be wrong.

Avoiding taking a decisive action for too long becomes, itself, a decision. Will Rogers pointed out that, *Even if you're on the right track, you'll get run over if you just sit there.* And that kind of waffling both comes from and reinforces a sense of uncertainty about one's abilities.

The Pulitzer Prize winning news correspondent, Anne O'Hare McCormick, rightly noted that,

> *The percentage of mistakes in quick decisions is no greater than in long-drawn-out vacillations, and the effect of decisiveness itself makes things go and creates confidence.*

Or, as Ralph Waldo Emerson put it, *Once you make a decision, the universe conspires to make it happen.*

Have sufficient trust in yourself to make wrong decisions, being confident that you will learn from mistakes and get things right the next time around. In other words, have enough trust in yourself to be able to make a wrong decision with confidence, and enough wisdom to never make the same wrong decision twice.

Trusting yourself to make decisions is the way you will grow and eventually become wealthy no matter how many setbacks you encounter along the path; making wise and timely decisions is the way all of us self-made people have become successful.

I should add that trust in myself is indivisible from my trust in my Maker. After all, if we believe that He is the Creator then He is the one who bestows upon me the resources of intelligence, energy, and commitment that, after all, make me trustworthy.

I am able to understand the Apostle Paul's ringing affirmation, *I can do everything through Him who gives me strength.* And I know exactly what the psalmist, writing six centuries earlier, meant when he wrote, *By my God I can leap over a wall.*

What am I going to do to develop trust in myself?

The following steps will direct you towards coming to trust your abilities and decisions:

1. Recall at least one mistake that you have made in business in the past year—something that you would not do again if given a do-over.

2. Identify one or two activities that could protect you against making the same mistake in the future.

3. Step back and make sure that any principle you have uncovered doesn't contain some defensive quality that will hold you back from vigorously trying new things in the future and making future mistakes that really are required for learning and growth.

4. Repeat the steps for other mistakes that you can think of. Make trusting yourself a habit.

Do these things carefully and review them on occasion and you will increase your trust in yourself.

Principle #4 - Do the Right Thing No Matter What

I learned early in my life to do the right thing no matter what the cost. Part of my commitment to the principle of doing right comes from my firm belief in the cosmic reality that what goes around really does come around.

We should do good without reservation or hesitation. I'm willing to follow the admonition of John Wesley, one of history's great preachers:

> *Do all the good you can, by all the means you can, in all the ways you can, in all the places you can, at all the times you can, to all the people you can, as long as you ever can.*

If you aren't willing to embrace the philosophy of doing good at this radical level, at least make a decision right now to behave towards the other people involved in your business in the way that you would want them to behave towards yourself. Be honest in every dealing; be faithful to your word.

Somebody once said that integrity combined with faithfulness is a powerful force, and that combination has allowed good things to flow to me. There's nothing pragmatic about this, however; even if it costs me time and money I'm still going to do what's right. I absolutely agree with an old proverb that says, *Better to be poor than a liar.*

The thing we need to grasp with both mind and heart, however, is that poverty and dishonesty really aren't connected. But good people can become successful more easily than bad ones can.

Albert Einstein said, *Try not to become a man of success, but rather try to become a man of value.* To a large extent, success in life—the kind that really blesses us and blesses the people who are associated with our business—is actually a by-product of the *value* that Einstein was speaking of.

Doing the right thing plays an essential role in creating the trust that we must develop with people—including employees, vendors, customers, and clients—so that they will want to do business *with* us and for us.

The billionaire investor, Warren Buffett, who knows some things about people and about success, wrote:

> *I look for three things in hiring people. The first is personal integrity, the second is intelligence, and the third is a high energy level. But if you don't have the first, the other two will kill you.*

When I started my first service business the two teenagers who inherited the business from their father didn't want anything to do with the company. I made an agreement with them that I would run the business until they sold it and then I would start my own company someplace else.

I was obviously in a perfect position to take advantage of those two young people. I could have used their trusting ignorance to put a lot of money in my own pocket and there would have been no way possible for them to know what I was up to. But I worked as diligently for their success as I would have for my own.

I was living out a principle that Douglas Adams noted, *To give real service you must add something which cannot be bought or measured with money, and that is sincerity and integrity.*

The two young people recognized how honest and upfront I was with them so when they decided that they wanted to sell the business they kept me in the loop.

You've been so good to us, they said, *running the business, showing it to perspective buyers. We want you to continue to run the company until you can get the money to buy it from us.*

We live lives full of energy and passion and thus fulfill our purpose; always moving our passion in an upward direction.

What am I going to do to live an ethical life?

The Golden Rule of treating others as we would have them treat us exerts a powerful force in this world. Since that is so, we can keep ourselves straight by identifying and then imitating the behaviors that we prefer in others. The following steps will direct you towards learning to do the right thing:

1. In the choices and tasks facing you, ask yourself what behaviors you would honor if they were exhibited by those with whom you are working and doing business.

   What activities in these areas would you respect from your employees, your peers, your vendors, your customers, and clients? Be as specific as possible and then adjust your own decisions to mirror those behaviors.

2. Ask yourself in the choices facing you what behaviors you would despise if they were exhibited by those with whom you are working.

What activities would alienate you and cause you to want to fire employees, or discontinue doing business with vendors, customers, and clients?

Be as specific as possible and then adjust your own decisions to avoid those behaviors.

3. Repeat the above two steps on a regular basis. Make ethical behavior a habit.

Principle #5 - Learn to Win by Staying Within the Lines

All of us entrepreneurs believe in the old adage that *Rules are made to be broken*. You always think how to do things differently and better than the *rules* say they should be done.

However, breaking rules becomes a negative and harmful behavior when we're breaking the rules governing moral and ethical behavior. The *wise* Roman Emperor and Stoic philosopher, Marcus Aurelius, wrote, *Never esteem anything as of advantage to thee that shall make thee break thy word or lose thy self-respect.*

Things are right or wrong in this area because of the way the moral universe operates. We get ourselves on the good side of the universe and achieve good, or we get ourselves on the wrong side and experience frustration and loss—no matter how much money breaking the rules achieved for us in the short term.

The Major League Baseball (MLB) drug scandal has caused real grief on the part of sports fans and ethical athletes alike. It has thrown the entire sport into chaos. A statistician examining records from MLB athletes divided the players into two chronological periods—Pre-steroid and Steroid.

We all understand the temptation that players face. Winning was the most important thing in their lives, and steroids offered them a means whereby they could move from mediocre to good, or from good to great, or from great to awesome.

Performance-enhancing drugs offer an irresistible shortcut to people who are as strongly motivated as these professional athletes are. Their big mistake—and one made by many highly motivated people—lay in the misunderstanding of the moral nature of the universe. Those pills that many players took did not ensure their success but, rather, guaranteed many of their failures. They could have been great without them. Perhaps not awesome (We'll never know that, of course.), but they would have been greater baseball players—revered, honored, and held up as persons to be celebrated and imitated.

Drugs brought many of them down; they ensured ultimate failure.

The story of the baseball players who were caught up in the scandal, provides a fitting illustration of a universal principle. Virtue is a requirement for ultimate success. In the final assessment true winners never cheat and cheaters never truly win.

Of course, the temptation is always strong for wrong-hearted people to believe that they can cheat and not get caught—that the players were simply unlucky enough to become trapped in an anti-drug sweep. But they were, in fact, trapped by their own weakness; lacking sufficient moral strength to bring their actions into alignment with the standards that would have made possible a place in history, even if they couldn't have ensured the highest place that they would not, in that case, have deserved.

Several of the players are enormously wealthy, but I'm sure when they look in the mirror—and when most people look at them, they're a failure who are dripping with money and are living proof that money provides no standard for success. No doubt their lives are with constant remorse over the decisions that they made that, though for a while they lifted them up physically, ultimately brought them crashing down.

Good and evil are dynamic qualities. The way you treat other people—whether in shabby and unworthy ways or in patterns that honor them and reflect your respect for them—infects the entire climate surrounding you. If your employees see you cutting corners and cheating customers, they will come to regard boundaries around their own jobs in ways that will not please you and that will detract from your possibility of success.

If, on the other hand, you treat your employees fairly and generously, their attitude towards you and towards the conduct of their job will be altered in ways that will promote the ability to conduct your business and to compete effectively in the marketplace.

And there's one other shining reality about right behavior of all kind: A number of people seem to believe that doing good is boring and drab; that pleasure is to be found in indulging our darker instincts because even ill-gotten wealth is a key to happiness. They believe that they can cheat themselves to contentment and fulfillment.

As a matter of fact, I've found just the opposite to be true. By *staying within the lines* in both business and my personal life, my cup has been running over with blessings. I've remained happy and fulfilled.

Nobody described what I'm talking about better than C.S. Lewis when he wrote the amazing paragraph:

> *Our Lord finds our desires not too strong, but too weak. We are half-hearted creatures, fooling about with drink and sex and ambition, when infinite joy is offered to us, like an ignorant child who wants to go on making mud pies in the slum because he cannot imagine what is meant by the offer of a holiday at the sea. We are far too easily pleased.*

Every day let's give ourselves to what is good, however we understand that to be, and let us do the right thing no matter what. Our days will then be filled with a good purpose that will bless the lives of others as it blesses our own lives. And through that purpose we will be able to earn wealth for ourselves, for our family, and to share with others as a means of helping serve the world and making it a better place.

What am I going to do to win in the right way?

The following steps will direct you towards learning to win by doing the right things in the right way:

1. What example can you think of in your life where you did something wrong to get something that you thought was right?

2. Identify one area today where you are tempted to take a short-cut—or are taking one.

   Consider the risks that belong to the shortcut—the unintended negative impact that your shortcut may be having upon the people around you—upon your own sense of self-worth.

3. Repeat these two steps on a regular basis. Make right moral behavior a habit.

Principle #6 - Get Focused

A proper focus will always move you towards the future and towards the goals that you have set for your life and for your business. We need to remember the past and not forget the lessons that we've learned and the mistakes that we've made. But the proper attention must be focused upon the current essential actions and decisions that will create success.

I tell my people that running our business is like driving a car. You need to look in the rear-view mirror from time to time just to remind yourself of what's behind you but, unless you're backing up, which you hopefully are not doing very often, looking forward through the windshield is infinitely more important than looking at the rear-view mirror.

You want to concentrate upon where you are going—the destination you are heading for—or you will never get there.

Novice entrepreneurs are tempted to make the error of trying to implement business tactics before they've identified business strategies. It makes no sense to search for office space or buy computers before you have clearly identified exactly what business you're going to conduct in that office or what data you are going to manage on those computers.

Great success requires continual reassessment of the opportunities at hand. Ron & Mary Hulnick, who authored *Financial Freedom in 8 Minutes a Day*, wrote, *What you focus on expands*. In other words, success only comes as we keep our purpose and the means of reaching that purpose always before our eyes.

We could illustrate the idea of focus with the simple example of using a powerful high-resolution camera lens. If it is your purpose, for example, to take a picture of a bird perched on a branch a hundred yards away, you want that telephoto lens to eliminate the river to one side, the mountains to the other, plus any surrounding buildings, trees, or bushes.

You want to be able to focus upon the object of your interest and let other things slide out of sight so that you've got the bird in your view to the exclusion of the other distractions. You would never use a wide-angle lens through which the bird becomes lost amid all the other objects—a cooling tower far over on the left, for example, or a marina far to the right—that are also in your field of vision. The bird is out there somewhere but becomes lost in the surrounding non-essential details.

Once you focus upon where you are going and what you are trying to accomplish other decisions come seemingly by themselves. One lesson Charlie Clark, my first mentor, drummed into me was, *Know where you're going and decisions will be easy for you.* I've learned that he spoke the truth.

Unfortunately, many businesses fail—sometimes following years of success—because, for some reason, the people running the business forgot about what they were doing and lost their focus. Perhaps they were focusing on their competitors, upgrading their HR benefits, providing programs of employee continuing education, etcetera. Note that all these things are good but should never take the place of essential operations.

I learned of a LAN manufacturing company that, decades ago, had the contract for networking in Microsoft's central office space. A friend of mine who worked for the LAN company said that, in speaking with a Microsoft engineer, he learned that Microsoft was experiencing equipment failures and that the LAN company wasn't returning repeated calls for service.

If you are a LAN service provider and you have the contract with Microsoft, what in the world is more important than keeping that client happy? The company had completely lost focus about what was important and even essential to their business.

'The good' is an enemy of 'The best,' they say. I suppose the account reps from the LAN company would have had what seemed to them good excuses for ignoring the problems at Microsoft, but there are no good excuses for such failure.

It was no surprise that the LAN company lost the contract and in a few years went out of business altogether.

Sometimes you have to go the extra mile, sometimes you have to burn the midnight oil, sometimes you have to leave undone other things that would have been good to do.... The foundational policy for any successful company has to be *Whatever it takes...*when it comes to providing core products and services. Success comes only when focus remains intense and unwavering.

What am I going to do to become and remain focused?

The essence of the issue is to focus upon the core things that are essential to your success. The following will help you to concentrate upon essential tasks:

1. Make a list of all the activities that belong to your business. Make this list as complete as possible.
2. Perform a rough assessment of how much time you spend on each of these—you can make this either a percentage of all your work or hours-per-week.
3. Assign each activity a place in the following chart.

    Note that the chart below has four quadrants. They would be labeled in the following way:

    Urgent/Important

    Urgent/Non Important

    Not Urgent/Important

    Not Urgent/Non Important

    Think about where you would place each of the activities you identified.

	Important	Non Important
Urgent		
Not Urgent		

4. Check out any activities you assign to the bottom-left quadrant. These Not Urgent/Important tasks are the ones that will require your focus because they are the ones that you can let slide thus causing problems.

You are probably attending to the activities in the top-left quadrant; most likely taking care of activities like Meeting Payroll.

You shouldn't care about activities in the bottom-right quadrant. You can let the Urgent/Non Important things go without going broke. If you forget to renew your subscription to a trade journal, for example, you'll still be all right. If you don't get the pothole in your driveway paved this month, you won't go broke.

Remember focus on the things in the bottom-left quadrant—the Not Urgent/Important. No one is going to fine you if you don't get proper rest and exercise, for example. Those things are Not Urgent but if you don't attend to them you are apt to lose your business and your health.

There's no urgent deadline to acknowledging good performance by one of your employees or splendid loyalty by one of your clients, but you will never enjoy brilliant success unless you do this.

Make a fearless inventory of your business needs and activities—from the inside out and from the top down. Deliberately identify those things that rightfully belong in that Not Urgent/Important quadrant. Focus every day upon those activities because they are the ones that will most likely spell the difference between success and failure in your business.

Principle #7 - Become Flexible

It's as important to be flexible as it is to be focused. The eminent U.S. Senator, Everett Dirksen, once observed, *I am a man of fixed and unbending principles, the first of which is to be flexible at all times.*

The role that flexibility and dynamic response to change can play in business success can be compared to panning for gold in a mountain stream. I live in Northern California and have neighbors and friends with placer sites along streambeds in the nearby Sierra Foothills—the so-called Gold Country.

During times of drought these sites can get worked out. When carried on too long, business-as-usual gold-panning activities can become barren. However, let a tremendous rush of water come sweeping down the stream from melting snows on the high peaks above and every-thing changes. Sandbars are swept away, the rushing waters gouge out new stream formations, islands disappear and others reappear.

The fierce changes provide opportunities for the people with their gold pans to discover new sources of wealth that previously had remained hidden beneath the stream or embedded in a riverbank that has now been uncovered.

We should be like those gold miners. When changes come ripping through our marketplace—as they surely will come—rather than lament over the things that have been carried away, we begin searching among the changed environment to discover new opportunities that hadn't been available only a few weeks or months before.

I got into service based businesses when a flood of people were migrating to our area from nearby Silicon Valley and San Francisco looking for inexpensive housing and creating a swelling tide of humanity. Each of those new families, of course, provided potential customers for my business. I accommodated my sales approach to respond to every new subdivision that opened up.

Imagine an example from the past: If you are in the business of manu-facturing buggy whips and people are suddenly driving around in auto-mobiles, simply figure out how to make the best windshield wipers that can be found anywhere. More people will be using windshield wipers in five years than ever used buggy whips five years before.

The influx of new residents in my area exerted tremendous pressures on local farmers. Land prices were going through the roof, causing many growers to sell out to developers. Farm supplies became more difficult to find. The big wholesalers were dropping commodity prices because of the pressure from the huge farm factories and foreign growers.

Most farmers considered the situation a lamentable mess. However, just like a rush of melt water through a placer mine from a distant snow-field, the changing environment carried with it wonderful new opportu-nities for local farmers if they only could learn how to identify and capitalize on the new opportunities that were being created.

One potential resource for wealth—that should have been more obvious than it was for some of the farmers—lay in viewing the huge influx of new residents as a marketing resource. By implementing an aggressive advertising campaign with direct farm-to-table marketing processes, we could eliminate the middleman, who customarily kept most of the profits. In that way we could tap this huge reserve of potential customers and lift our farming community to unimagined heights.

I worked on encouraging the local farmers' association to push our lo-cally-grown products to our community residents as well as to the other burgeoning Northern California communities. I worked with a Downtown Business Association in order to create a multi-pronged marketing effort designed at getting products from local fields, trees, and bushes onto the tables of local residents.

Another possibility for utilizing the market represented by the inflow of new residents lay in creating boutique quality farms and farm products. To that end I planted groves of olive trees and began bottling my olive oil for sale into the fast-growing networks of restaurants and specialty shops. Some of my wine-growing neighbors are planning to build wine tasting rooms.

There's a lot of energy in any change, even one that seems to most people to be negative. Be flexible. Look for ways to leverage any change for your own benefit.

What am I going to do to remain flexible?

The essence of flexibility is to respond to change in ways that will create positive energy for you to use in building up your business. The following steps will direct you towards preparing for and accommodating yourself and your business to changing circumstances:

1. List the five most dramatic changes that have impacted or might impact your business.

2. Think of three ways that you might respond to each of those five changes—finding potential to leverage each change by re-thinking how you do your business.

3. Plan to implement your responses in creating new business practices that transform change into profits.

4. Revisit this exercise on a regular basis. Make flexibility a habit.

Principle #8 - Live in the Present

We need to remember lessons from the past and make plans for the future but the present is where we live and in this moment we are creating either success or failure.

About the future C.S. Lewis wrote, *Nearly all vices are rooted in the future. Gratitude looks to the past and love to the present; fear, avarice, lust, and ambition look ahead.*

Mark Twain made the famous comment about undue concern over the future, *I've had a lot of problems in my life most of which never happened.*

Concerning the past, I'm following the advice of Charles Dickens, who wrote, *Reflect upon your present blessings, of which every man has plenty; not on your past misfortunes, of which all men have some.*

In an even more profound way the Indian spiritual leader and humanitarian, with the tongue-twisting name of Mātā Amritanandamayī, wrote:

> The past can be compared to a graveyard, and it wouldn't be wise to live in such a place, would it? Forget your past. Remember it only when you really need to do so, but don't settle down in it.

I had a lot of difficulties as a young boy—motherless when I was five and close to penniless at 18. It would be easy to be resentful and bitter about the bad hand that my past had dealt me. I can remember insults and slights. But what good would it ever do to hold to myself the memory of any of those bad experiences?

In the same way, I'm always facing a lot of problems as I move into the future—aggravations, some of which, if not handled properly, will turn into disasters.

I've learned to focus on personal challenges, which means letting go of things from the past that might make me worried or hesitant. And not becoming distracted by concerns over the future that subject me to needless worry or to the *avarice, lust, and ambition* that C.S. Lewis wrote about.

An acquaintance of mine was engaged in a risky enterprise that, if it succeeded, promised to earn him a lot of money in a few months, but would create economic disaster if it failed.

The man's wife was greatly agitated about the risk involved and every day would remind the man of the awful potential that waited for them if their hopes didn't pan out.

The man finally told his wife, *If we end up a year from now with more money in the bank than we ever before imagined having, you will owe me an apology for trying to bring down my spirit.*

Then he continued, *But if the project collapses and a year from now we're living in a van down by the river, I will never wish that I had been able to worry more.*

Take appropriate steps to guard against problems that might arise. Keep your insurance payments up to date, but don't spend energy fretting about anything that might possibly happen. Mary Hemingway, who was a journalist, (and Ernest Hemingway's fourth wife) pointed out an important truth:

Worry a little bit every day and in a lifetime you will lose a couple of years. If something is wrong, fix it if you can. But train yourself not to worry. Worry never fixes anything.

The other part of focusing inordinately upon the future is to continually build dream castles and then be so caught up in hopes and plans that you lose focus of the satisfactions and fulfillment of the charms and gifts of the present. In his *Screwtape Letters,* C.S. Lewis put words into an arch-demon's mouth about this topic as the demon spoke about a technique for bringing mankind down to ruin:

We want a whole race perpetually in pursuit of the rainbow's end, never honest, nor kind, nor happy now, but always using as mere fuel wherewith to heap the altar of the Future every real gift which is offered them in the Present.

Every morning I get out of bed, greet the new day, and with great enthusiasm I begin working on the tasks that are waiting for me. I'm not going to be stalled by things from the past that are dead and gone. I'm not going to be confused by problems and possible eventualities from the future, I'm going to live and work in the present. This is where I will find my success.

It just doesn't make good sense to live any other way.

What am I going to do to live and work in the present?

The following steps will direct your attention away from regrets and failures of the past and undue concern for the future:

1. Make a list of all the things from the past that bother you and that hinder you from enjoying life and distract you from concentrating on the present.

a. Wad the paper up and, in some safe place, burn it.

b. Deliberately let your feelings of disappointment and resentment go up in the smoke.

2. Make a list off all the things that you are concerned about in the future. Write them in two columns labeled *Things that I have control over* and *Things I have no control over.*

a. Resolve to fix the things you have control over so that you won't have to worry over them.

b. Resolve not to worry over the things you have no control over, since no amount of worry will ever change a thing.

Principle #9 - Concentrate on Excellence, Not Profits

The bottom line in my businesses remains strong in part because I don't worry about the money itself. The best kinds of profits are those that come as by-products of the base of quality and customer service that I build into my businesses. My goal is to provide service for every customer at what somebody called *a Wow! level.* Focusing upon my clients' best interests is no slogan or marketing phrase; it is a principle that I live by.

I recently learned about the performance of a man who owned a cesspool cleaning service. A man who lived in a rural area without urban utilities told the story of how his sewer system was overflowing. The service man, who obviously took great pride in his humble work, pumped out the pool, rinsed it down several times, and continued rinsing and pumping until the cesspool was shining clean. He made sure to call the owner to inspect the results of his efforts and obviously took great pride in his work.

If I lived in that area and had a cesspool I would use the services of this man and would never check prices with anyone else for a competitive bid. Obviously, a cesspool will work just as well if it is slimy and grimy as it will shiny clean, but the experience of getting it cleaned out is different when conducted by a person with a goal of excellence.

Along the same lines, I learned of a man who ran a firewood business. He took great pride in cutting each piece to an exact length and then stacking the firewood in perfectly neat cords. He would deliver wood to clients in impeccably neat stacks and filled his yard every fall with great woodpiles each aligned in perfect symmetry with adjoining piles and each length of wood in precise alignment with the others in the stack.

A friend called one night and told his wife, *Tell Jack to get out into his yard. I just drove by and saw a single piece of wood that was crooked. He better straighten it up.*

The story earned a well-deserved laugh but the fact is that if I was in that man's area and had a fireplace or a wood-burning stove, I would buy wood from him. Obviously, wood doesn't burn any better if it is taken off a neat stack or picked out of a jumbled pile, but the experience is different.

The issue is more than one of mere experience; I want to do business with people who concentrate on excellence. If they obviously excel in any part of the business that I can see—how clean a cesspool is or how straight the rows of wood in a yard—then I can have confidence that they will be excellent in the other parts of the business that are less obvious.

For example, I can easily imagine that the cesspool cleaner will not try to slip in a charge not covered by the contract-for-service; I can easily believe that the man with the firewood won't be trying to slip some rotten or inferior wood into my order, hoping I will not notice the trick that he pulled—or only notice when it's too late.

If you concentrate upon excellent service the money will come later. Make it your goal to become the ambassador of this principle in front of your staff. Model excellence by the way you treat customers yourself. Treat your staff excellently, as well. Show them how to *exceed customer expectations.*

You can never build a great business on price point alone. The author, poet, and artist, John Ruskin, correctly observed, *There is scarcely anything in the world that some man cannot make a little worse, and sell a little more cheaply. The person who buys on price alone is this man's lawful prey.*

You can be assured that you'll never create a business by making something *a little worse*, that you then *sell a little more cheaply*. You can get away with that by making cheaper toothpicks or paper clips, perhaps, but those types of product lines aren't amenable to the efforts of young entrepreneurs no matter how creative or energetic.

You will succeed in business by providing service of an standard far beyond the shabby and ineffective customer service that has become a byword in our modern American culture or by creating excellent quality products. Figure this out, do this right, and you'll have good leverage for snatching and eating your competitors' lunch. They won't know what hit them!

Don't just create another *computer*. Be a Steve Jobs. Do something *insanely great*. The principle holds equally well if you build a woodpile as it does for building the next Macintosh.

What am I going to do to concentrate on excellence?

The following steps will direct you towards preparing for excellence in your life and your business:

1. List all the points at which your business intersects with your customers and clients. Imagine that you were a customer.... What would you think about the quality of your customer care?

2. Every month or two call up your own business or get an acquaintance to do this for you. Pretend that you are a customer or client. Ask some questions about the business—your products or service. How polite were your people? How efficiently did they get the answers you need? Did they seem genuinely interested in you or did they give the impression that your call was just a bother?

3. Schedule regular follow-up calls to your clients or to customers who purchased products from you. Ask them how satisfied they are...and how likely they are to do repeat business with you.

4. Make a plan based upon the findings from the three points above to address any problems you uncover. Make this recursive: ensure that the changes actually fixed the problems.

5. Repeat the four steps above on a regular basis. Make excellence a habit.

Principle #10 - Expect to Fail Forward to Success

One of the key principles for anyone wishing to become successful includes the attitudes and strategies for coping with failure. Mary Kay Ash, founder of Mary Kay Cosmetics, made the observation that *people fail forward to success.* Wise and successful people are never those who avoid making mistakes, but are people who learn from their mistakes.

In terms of sheer numbers, Thomas Edison must have been one of the greatest failures who ever lived. After he had failed 700 times to find a filament for the light bulb, a bold young reporter asked Mr. Edison if he felt like a failure. Edison's famous reply comes as a call to anyone who pursues success:

> *I have not failed 700 times. I have not failed once. I have succeeded in proving that those 700 ways will not work. When I have eliminated all the ways that will not work, I will find a way that will work.*

Dr. David M. Burns, Professor of Psychiatry and Behavioral Sciences at the Stanford University, made the wise observation:

> *We all fail many times. Failures are those who don't push pass the failure to the success that lies beyond. Aim for success, not perfection. Never give up your right to be wrong, because then you will lose the ability to learn new things and move forward with your life.*

A success coach named Jennifer White put it most succinctly when she wrote, *Fail often to succeed sooner.*

Failure has played an important role in my own success. I ran in one of my first trail races at age 25, after training religiously for three months. I thought that I was prepared for the 13-mile trail run through some Northern California hills. After running about four miles into the race, a 60-year-old woman passed me while going up a hill. As she went by she turned to me and said, in a voice that I'm sure was intended to be comforting, *Boy! These hills are tough.*

The comment and her passing me on the trail took the wind right out of my sails. I ended limping across the finish line in dead last place. Some of the other competitors were already packing up their equipment and rolling out of camp by the time I arrived.

I'm not used to failure—particularly failure of that appalling magnitude and I spent a few depressed days before finally talking myself out of the funk that I had fallen into. I realized that I couldn't go in any direction except up from that point, so I reset my goals and used the negative energy created by that awful experience as a basis for making improvement the next time out.

We can learn to use failures as a springboard to get past barriers and on to success. In fact, Wayne Dyer has accurately pointed out that, *Nothing fails like success because you do not learn anything from it. The only thing we ever learn from is failure.*

Not everybody learns from failures, of course. The single quality, perhaps, that marks skid row derelicts and other life-long failures is that they, somehow, were never able to derive benefit or learn lessons from their personal disappointments and catastrophes.

Experience grows out of mistakes and errors.

"How do you get good judgment?" runs the first line of an old joke.

"By experience," is the answer.

"How do you get experience?"

"By bad judgment."

This goes right along with a profound insight: *Mistakes are painful when they happen*, Denis Watley, a psychologist, admitted, *but years later a collection of mistakes is what is called experience.* In the same vein he wrote:

> *When you make a mistake or get ridiculed or rejected, look at mistakes as learning experiences, and ridicule as ignorance.... Look at rejection as part of one performance, not as a turn down of the performer.*

The same Denis Watley also wrote a passage that sums up the whole principle:

Failure should be our teacher, not our undertaker. Failure is delay, not defeat. It is a temporary detour, not a dead end. Failure is something we can avoid only by saying nothing, doing nothing, and being nothing.

Never make any decision because you fear failure. Embrace failure as a means of learning and progressing on your way to success.

What am I going to do to learn to turn failure into success?

Everyone makes mistakes; just learn what you can from the things you experience and move on. Be deeply afraid, however, of ever making the same mistake twice. The following steps will help you face up to and profit from failure and protect you from repeated errors:

1. Write down an error you have made during the past three months.
2. Write down as specifically as you can something you might have known or should have done that would have prevented the mistake from happening.
3. Write down 1–3 lessons that you learned from the mistake.
4. Repeat the above three steps with all the errors that you can think of that have been bothering you.
5. Repeat the three steps every time you make a mistake. Get in the habit of deliberately tracking the lessons that you learn from the mistakes that you make.

Chapter 5: Principles About Becoming a Successful You

6 Principles About Learning to be Successful

Many of us young entrepreneurs believe that we know it all because we haven't yet learned what we don't know. We need to remain in a learning mode throughout our lives. Even if you have your current situation figured out, you can know for certain that the future will bring changes that you better be ready to learn about and thus be able to accommodate.

Learning is the avenue that permits growth in skills that lead to exceptional success. An old adage tells us that, *What you don't know won't kill you*. I don't know if that's true in any important area but it is certainly untrue when it comes to the conduct of business. Your business can die a sure and horrible death if you aren't able to learn the things that will continue to give it life.

John Marsh, the man who built the first pioneer home in my area—erected the stone house only five miles from my home, in fact—was a lifelong learner who said that, *Poverty and ignorance go hand in hand*.

Make it your goal to acquire the marketing information you need. Remain on top of the game when it comes to your competition; remain alert to the vagaries of your market niche; continue to learn how to do your business better.

Technology moves so rapidly in every area of business and commerce that, unless we remain abreast, we soon discover that the world has moved on and we have become stranded by advances in the area of marketing, product development, and service delivery.

Whether for good or bad—and a lot of it is good—the coming of the Internet changed everything forever. An acquaintance of mine attended a business and technology show. He visited the kiosk that was being run by the company that was putting on the show. One of the people in the booth pointed to a computer that was running the company's website.

All the vendors in this show will be on the website, she said. *It is a virtual industry show.* My friend noted that the effect of the website might be that the company would put its shows out of business.

The woman laughed and said, *Our Vice President maintains that we're in the process of eating our own children.*

And then she added, somewhat more soberly, *The woman says that if we don't eat them ourselves then our competitors surely will.*

Technology is just one example of the areas in which all businesspeople have to continually be learning about what they are doing. New techniques are being devised for doing things. Innovative methods are being discovered for streamlining processes that were formerly laborious and resource-consuming. Products are continually being developed to work in more efficient and in effective ways.

No industry that I know of is exempt from these pressures—certainly all the industries that will enable you to acquire wealth in a relatively short length of time experience these changes.

You might imagine that washing windows would be a relatively stable and unchanging business. However, I know of a man with a highly successful window washing business who subscribes to two journals that are centered on the window washing industry.

The man is always working on his website, developing new processes for coordinating with others in his business, and working as a third-party reseller of window-washing products. He is happy and thriving. He's been doing this for two decades and has learned things about his business in the past six weeks that he never realized before—discovered products he didn't know about, and learned about techniques that were new to him. The window washing industry is a constantly unfolding and exciting entity as far as that man is concerned.

You could have a window washing business without doing any of these things but you would never grow the business into a source of wealth without doing all of these.

You will have a leg up on the competition and a good prospect for success in your business if you follow the advice of Henry Doherty:

> Get over the idea that only children should spend their time in study. Be a student so long as you still have something to learn, and this will mean all your life.

George Boas, a renowned professor of philosophy, noted that, *Education is learning what you didn't know you didn't know.* This is one of the curious and great advantages of remaining in a learning mode. Some 13-year-old kids believe that they know everything because of their ignorance concerning the existence of a vast universe of information.

An anonymous wise man added, *Although ignorance is not bliss, the greatest enemy of knowledge is not ignorance but the illusion of knowledge.* In other words, learning begins with the realization that you in fact have things you need to know.

Acknowledged ignorance can be remedied; ignorance unaware of itself is deadly. *He who knows not and knows not that he knows not is a fool. Shun him!* That is a great piece of advice.

Learn everything you can about whatever industry you are in. Subscribe to relevant trade journals. Talk to everyone in the business. Go to trade shows and listen carefully to what's being said. Visit showrooms. Learn about your competitors' products and services. Buy stock in a large public company in your field. Learn what they are doing and then do it better. Use the Internet to discover the latest industry information. Seek to become a specialist in your field. Don't go to bed without having learned something new during the day that can help move you to success.

I'm a life-long learner. It's the only way to continue to thrive. Henry Ford made a wise observation: *Anyone who stops learning is old, whether at twenty or eighty.* By that standard I intend to remain young forever.

Principle #11 - Learn What You Need to Prepare for Success

There is no substitution for careful preparation. You have to do a lot of intelligent groundwork before you are able to run any business. I would have failed miserably running my service-based companies if I hadn't spent two years diligently paying attention to every part of that business.

Four out of five businesses fail within the first year because too many people think that, with nothing but an idea and a catchy name or a cool logo, they can jump into a business and make it work on sheer creativity. Such delusional people are doomed to failure.

Of course, with enough stubbornness and sufficient available resources, in the absence of careful preparation some people can fail their way to success by continually learning from their mistakes. Those kinds of resources and that kind of person are rare, however. Most ill-prepared people simply end up eventually working for someone else. That kind of learning that is limited to *the school of hard knocks* is difficult and wasteful.

With any business I begin, before looking for the first customer, I determine the stages that the business will go through, document the levels of anticipated growth, and identify the resources that will get us to each stage. Before beginning some businesses I also identify an exit strategy—the point at which I will divest myself of the business and move on to other things.

Success comes most naturally through processes of due diligence. Becoming a specialist—understanding everything about every part of the business—doesn't ensure success, but lack of this detailed knowledge will guarantee failure.

I had to find the rhythm and grow each business one step at a time. Adequate preparation—from skills development to the creation of a business plan—contributes to the level of respect and trust you can expect from others. It doesn't matter how winning your personality is or how much integrity you have, people will turn away from you if you lack sufficient preparation to succeed at your business.

You must develop the habit of paying attention to the details about any business venture you enter into, gathering and analyzing data and information. You need to discipline yourself to take the time to do this preparation step correctly.

Such discipline requires patience that doesn't come easy to some of us—especially those of us with A-type personalities and perhaps more than a touch of concomitant ADD. We prefer to be like Star Trek's Captain Picard and simply tell someone else, *Make it so*. Or, as some of us caught up in the New Age culture like to word it, *Just handle it for me*.

But the fact is, especially at the beginning of a company's life, when the entrepreneurial style is in most demand (as opposed to the executive officer types required in larger and more established organizations), we must be prepared to do the thing ourselves—or at least prepare ourselves with the knowledge of exactly what the task actually requires for success.

What am I going to do to prepare myself for success?

The following steps will help you implement processes of preparation for any business undertaking:

1. Set aside a block of time each week with a mentor—some successful business person who is willing to spend time in helping you become successful.
2. Every week show your mentor your accomplishments from the week before and your plans for the coming week.
3. Do a reality check each week with your mentor—measuring your accomplishments against the goals you have set for yourself. Make any changes indicated.
4. Don't become lazy about this and let it slip. Get into the habit of always planning for success.

Principle #12 - Tackle the Unknown Head On

Unless you are born with a silver spoon in your mouth or win the lottery, success will never come easy. We in the generation of emerging leaders must acquire the habit of tackling the things that we fear or that we are ignorant of head on.

Learning is an area for boldness and not timidity. We should seek to acquire the attitude of a legendary lieutenant in the Civil War who called out to his troops in the midst of a terrible battle, *It looks like they have us surrounded, boys! So don't let a one of 'em escape!*

We should cultivate that kind of attitude about things we need to improve on as a business professional and then *just do it!*

I absolutely agree with a comment by Robert Louis Stevenson, *You cannot run away from a weakness; you must sometimes fight it out or perish.* He followed that up with an excellent question, *And if that be so, why not now, and where you stand?*

When I began in business I feared the unknown and was terrified of the mistakes that my ignorance might lead me to make. So I would make a list of my five biggest fears on a sheet of paper and then take deliberate steps to overcome them.

For example, bookkeeping was one of the original five things that I feared. I didn't know anything about it and was afraid of the harm that my ignorance could cause. So I focused on bookkeeping tasks and taught myself by asking questions and spending time with my bookkeeper. In that way I acquired sufficient proficiency to be able to read a ledger or a P & L statement and understand exactly what was going on.

Other personal deficiencies that I uncovered in those early years included skills ranging from creating PowerPoint presentations, on one hand, and learning company payroll processes, taxes, etcetera on the other.

After gaining the knowledge and skills required in an area, I would move on and master the required skills in another. In this way I quickly grew my ability to master the challenges of my business and manage people more effectively. After all, you can't manage people when you have no idea what they do or how they do it.

The goal in this learning is to convert areas of weakness into areas of strength. If you are really fearful about speaking in front of people, for example, join the local Toastmasters Club. Make it your purpose to win the blue ribbon every time you are the club speaker. Resolve to improve your skills until you become a sought-after public speaker.

If you have to work with employees or clients who do not speak your native language, find a way to learn the language, using books, tapes, or simply being around the language spoken. Resolve in a year to become the most competent bi-lingual team member in the company.

I can't tell you how important this principle is. Most people want to avoid areas that they are ignorant about; to stay away from areas of weakness. They concentrate their energies only in those areas that they are comfortable with. Work hard to overcome this tendency in your own life.

I've continued with my mastery activities every year until the present—each year making a list of skills that I need to acquire and subjects that I need to learn. In that way I grow better all the time; each year the things that I fear and the areas that I'm ignorant about become fewer and less important.

What am I going to do to aggressively face up to areas of fear or ignorance?

The following steps will help you identify and respond to areas in which you need to ramp up your knowledge:

1. Make a list of the five areas of ignorance that you are most concerned about.
2. Devise a plan to remedy each of those conditions.
3. For the entire year, focus on acquiring knowledge and skills in those areas.
4. At the end of the year, choose five other areas in which you are ignorant and fearful. Make continual learning a habit.

Principle #13 - Identify Your Market

There are winners and losers in any marketplace. And the winners invariably are those with the most detailed information about where their market is and who their clients and customers are.

I've been a member of the local farm scene in my area since I was just a pup. Farming was never an easy avenue to wealth. They tell the story of two farmers sitting on a bench outside a feed store. One of them asks the other, "What would you do if someone gave you a million dollars?" The other answered, "Same thing I'm doing now as long as the money held out."

Changing conditions have led to the failure of many local farms, sometimes after generations of working the land. Part of the problem is that people lost their market. Competition from the big factory farms and offshore imports of farm goods took the heart out of the traditional market.

I'm thriving in my business, however, because I'm identifying new, pre-viously-untapped markets. Instead of selling my olives and my olive oil to the huge processors and to the global distributors, I'm selling my products to people right here in Northern California where I live.

And I'm leading an effort to help other local olive growers, wine growers, and farmers reach into this potentially lucrative market.

Everything is changing in our part of the county and one of the great changes that has been taking place over the past decade or so is the growth of the wine industry. A large number of vineyards are springing up and local varietals are garnering prizes in regional, national, and even international competitions.

Most residents in my area have never gotten the memo that some of the best products in the state are right here in their back yards. They aren't aware of the award-winning wines and olive oils that are grown within a 20-minute drive. Our local cherries, corn, wines, oils, and peaches, are some of the best that money can buy. We're on the top of the food chain with our local-grown products.

Since we couldn't stop the wheels of progress from continuing to grind, even if we wished to do so, the alternative is to manage the processes of change in order to maintain a space for area agriculture to continue to thrive regardless of whatever else is happening to the society around us. We must create changes in strategy and directions that will enable us to continue to thrive in this life that we have come to love.

These new residents, with all their expendable income, become the marketplace for our farm products. I'm going to thrive in my business because I know who those people are. I'm learning about their tastes and about their buying patterns. I'm discovering what media are effective in selling products and services to them.

Get in the habit of looking carefully at the market for your products or services. See who else is out there. Learn what avenues successful people around you are using to sell into the market.

In 1943, Thomas Watson, who was then Chairman of IBM, made the astonishing comment, *I think there is a world market for maybe five computers*. What a laugh that was, in retrospect, since I have five computers in my home! IBM was standing at the threshold of what would be one of the greatest markets in the history of buying and selling. And they made billions, of course, because they soon came to understand where that market was and what impact their computers could have.

We need to be like IBM. Learn where our market is and understand the impact that our products and services can have.

What am I going to do to identify my marketplace?

The following steps will help you in identifying the market for your products and services:

1. Make a list of all the categories of people who are your clients or customers.
2. Find the demographics about them—age, average incomes, spending patterns.
3. Search for other groups of people—potential customers who may have been under the radar.
4. Plan for new marketing strategies to meet all these people.
5. Do these steps periodically. Make it a habit to know your market.

Principle #14 - Find New Ways of Providing Products and Service

In any industry a bell curve could be drawn to represent the earning power and profitability of people in the industry. A few people on the left side of the curve will be amazingly profitable, a few on the right side of the curve will be failing, the majority of people in the middle will be doing okay.

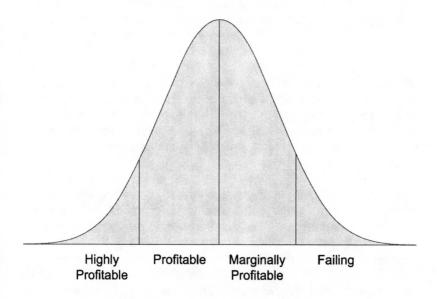

Highly Profitable	Profitable	Marginally Profitable	Failing

Figure 2: Bell Curve of Profitable Industries

Farming in America—and perhaps worldwide—has fallen on hard times. But I'm beginning to thrive because I've found new ways of getting my products into consumers' hands. I'm moving towards the left side of the Bell curve.

Several years ago I launched into a new industry by planting several groves of olive trees on my property. By the third year I began to harvest crops of olives, selling them to producers and creating my own label of extra virgin olive oil.

Some of my neighbors that hope to emulate my business model have begun planting olive groves of their own. Micro-farms are springing up around me and we have built goodwill and a strong demand for local products.

We're putting the financial power associated with economy of scale to good use and are adopting strategies and processes that will greatly expand our revenue streams. For one thing, we're building an olive press for our own crops and will provide pressing service for other area olive growers.

A commercial press involves considerable expense but the press can be repurposed for grapes as well as for olives so we'll have the opportunity to serve members of the extensive and growing local wine industry.

We are on the way to becoming the premier Northern California resource for premium olives and olive oil. We're investing resources of time, money, and energy in making this happen. We are building for sure success on the market research we carried out that led to the development of a comprehensive plan of action. We are now executing the plan.

One of our major tasks is to create a strategy of getting our local restaurateurs to use our oils in their cooking and, in fact, the majority of local area restaurants are. This has represented real progress because only a couple years ago almost none of them were. We feel we can compete with Italian olive oils and beat them at their own game.

One problem is that only twenty percent of the olive oil consumed in the U.S. is grown domestically. Plus, even though olive oil is becoming more popular, it still lags behind countries in Europe where olive oil comprises 80 percent of all cooking oils. In America the percentage is just reversed: 80 percent of the cooking we do is based upon vegetable oil.

I'm doing things to educate people concerning the advantages of our products. Olive oil costs about the same as other oils, for example, but it is much healthier for you and tastes far better. The U.S. is starting to adopt standards against trans-fats so Americans should increase their use of olive oil as a way of adapting themselves to healthier eating.

This type of approach to olive oil marketing practices provide an example of finding a product, developing a marketing strategy, and taking advantage of an opportunity.

I'll guarantee that there are better ways of selling whatever products or services you are dealing with; people who don't know how good you are; whole population groups that would buy from you if only you knew how to reach them—to position your products and services so that they will come and buy them.

If you creatively search for new ways of providing products and services, you will find them. One of the main differences between people who are on the right side of the bell curve chart of profitability and we who are on the far left side is that we've figured out how to do this.

What can I do to do to identify new ways of providing products and services?

The following steps will help you discover other means of selling your products. Get one or two people who know your business to help you with this, if you can:

1. Ask someone who knows your business to quickly list on a paper or a whiteboard ten other ways that you could possibly sell your products or services—new people you could sell to, or new ways you could market yourself.

2. Go through the list and pick out 1–3 most likely means of increasing your business.

3. Create a mini-marketing plan for each one you selected. Identify goals, resources, and marketing channels.

4. Implement the mini-marketing plan.

5. Go through these steps every time your business needs *a shot in the arm*. Make a habit of creating new marketing opportunities for yourself.

Principle #15 - Identify Recurring Revenue Streams

The best businesses are based upon a recurring revenue source—one that provides a residual pool of happy customers who keep returning on a regular basis for the products and/or services that you provide.

Almost any type of commercial enterprise that you start can be linked to some kind of recurring revenue stream. In some cases the profit margins will be less than your core business, but the payoff comes in the stable source of ongoing profits that they provide. Companies that develop this kind of multi-channel and ongoing revenue source become more recession-proof. So be prepared to trade profitability for stability.

For example, if you are a pool builder, then start a maintenance company to service the pools you build. Begin servicing pools that other companies have built. You may not make the big bucks from this as from selling pools, but the collateral business will cover your overhead when pool sales slow. The pool-maintenance side-business will help you weather economic downturns.

As another example, if you are selling gift baskets, then create a *Gift Basket of the Quarter Club*. As membership in the club increases the side business will become an important ongoing distribution channel. You will be sending products to your customers rather than simply waiting for them to come to you.

The ability to create these side businesses has become one of the key criteria that I use when analyzing companies that I'm considering becoming involved in.

Make it a point to always add ancillary services to anything you sell as a means of generating recurring revenue. For example, if you are marketing computers, you could add Tech Support, Training and Education, peripherals, on-site or remote backup services.

Some of these seem obvious, but think outside the box. You could also add a computer cleaning service, for example. Every month customers pay you to clean their computers until they glistened. Or you could add a quarterly *tune-up* service, where technicians would periodically go through the computer checking for corrupted files, viruses, duplicate applications, etcetera.

If you're selling automobiles, consider adding a side business that would detail the car on-site every six months.

If you're selling bicycles, consider adding a side business offering membership in a touring club, with local and distant destinations. For a fee your company would provide all the transportation, lodging, and dining accommodations.

We could go on with this giving examples from every kind of industry. You can continue with this considering side services you could provide—even setting up subsidiary companies to run the business.

Look at your core service or product-line with an eye to generating recurring business channels. Nearly every business affords the possibility of creating this kind of component.

What am I going to do to identify perpetual sources of income?

The following steps will help you discover income avenues that can create ongoing revenue streams:

1. List the products and services that you offer.
2. For each one, list as many associated services that you can think of.
3. Look at them from the customer or client's point of view. If you were doing business with your company, what other kind of product or service would you like to receive?

Principle #16 - Discover the Way of Discipline

The problem with most of us A-type personalities who do well in business is that our attention span is about as long as our pinky finger. We need to learn to provide necessary attention to required tasks.

To be an effective leader running a successful company, we must recognize the necessity of spending sufficient time looking at and analyzing details, and conducting the research that is a key component to running a successful operation.

Also, we need to be able to attend to the repetitive *grunge* work of finance, payroll, internal communications, advertising, client support tracking, sales and marketing; all those day-by-day tasks that aren't fun but, if ignored, will bring a business down in shambles.

Undisciplined creativity leads to disaster. Norman Podhoretz, a noted political theorist, noted that, *Creativity represents a miraculous coming together of the uninhibited energy of the child with its apparent opposite and enemy, the sense of order imposed on the disciplined adult intelligence.* Or, as Katharine Hepburn put it much more succinctly, *Without discipline, there's no life at all.*

You can establish effective discipline and attend to the ongoing details by simply turning what you need to do to be successful into a habit. For example, I know that I'm required to conduct a weekly, or sometimes even daily, financial forecast of our companies but this sometimes gets shoved aside by other pressing business matters. Or perhaps there are other things that I prefer doing.

But if I make it a habit to run the forecast every Monday at 10:30 a.m., for example, or every afternoon at 4 p.m., after a while I don't even think about it any more. I don't have to wonder whether I should do it, or not. I just do it. A deeply ingrained habit doesn't require as much effort as activities that are conducted on an ad hoc basis.

We will put in the requisite effort to establish these disciplines if we see the connection between the activities and the goals that we have established. If we care enough about what we're doing and about the goals we want to accomplish then we'll do whatever it takes to turn our vision into reality.

Sir Alexander Paterson said, *The secret of discipline is motivation. When a man is sufficiently motivated, discipline will take care of itself.*

Or as someone told me, *I'll do what other people won't do so that I can have what other people can't have.*

The good thing about habit is that if you simply undertake an action with faithful repetition then the habit just comes. *Do something every day for a month*, someone said, *and you will be able to do it forever.*

Also, I've learned how important discipline is for my own sense of self-worth. If I can't harness my appetites and inclinations that are contrary to my success, then I really am a weak person and not worthy of the success that I'm working for.

Self-respect is the fruit of discipline, Abraham Herschel, one of the 20th century's leading Jewish theologians, wrote, *The sense of dignity grows with the ability to say no to oneself*. He got that right.

What am I going to do to discipline myself in the right areas?

The following steps will help you exert discipline over your actions:

1. Make a list of all the things you want to do in the year ahead. You may use as a starting point my own list of disciplines above in *Chapter 3* - Get in the Habit of Success, but change these to fit your own set of purposes and goals.
2. Conduct your life by the goals. Write them down, put them somewhere they can't be missed, and check yourself against them every day.
3. Every year revise these goals and begin again to live by them. Create the habit of living a disciplined life.

There's a principle of unhelpfulness about this process. If you are struggling to conduct yourself in a disciplined fashion then it will be a struggle to maintain these goals. Get an accountability partner to help encourage you in this.

You are the only one who can move you into a life of discipline and growth. But know that there's a big payoff to succeeding in this.

Principle #17 - Learn What's Required to Grow to the Next Level

When I started my first company, one of the biggest frustrations was how to grow and get to the next level. Many companies hit a plateau that makes it difficult to keep growing. A variety of skills is required for managing a business bringing in a million dollars a year, and the skills differ greatly from those required for a company bringing in a hundred thousand dollars a year.

Many thriving companies come to ruin because the owner failed to realize that the skills that were so effective in growing the business were not sufficient to move the company beyond a certain level.

The issue kept me up at night many hours. I would lie awake in bed with my eyes wide open, staring at the ceiling, and thinking about how I was going to grow the business to the next plane of prosperity. (Does this sound familiar to you?)

I discovered that I possess the special kind of flexibility required to move a business into higher levels of operation and have overcome the plateau issue in various ways for the diverse businesses that I own.

Growing a business becomes another area in which planning is paramount. While you are still at the hundred thousand dollar a year level you need to begin envisioning your million-dollar company. What will you need at that point? What changes will you need to make in your distribution system? What changes in your management style? What other procedures will you need to put into place? At what point will you need to implement HR policies and processes?

These are complicated questions but none of this is rocket science. A lot of the answers will be found through books you read, journals you subscribe to, and industry-related conferences you attend.

The point is that you need to be continually reinventing yourself—acquiring new skills and increasing your knowledge in your industry niche. And acquiring the new knowledge and attitudes is a time-critical process; one you have to evaluate from quarter-to-quarter.

Don't be afraid about this or develop some kind of lazy or frustrated response. This is the kind of thing that we real entrepreneurs love to do. Who wants to do business-as-usual the rest of your life? That's the kind of 9-to-5 mentality we should resist. This continual change is what makes business fun. It is what we thrive on.

A word of wisdom about all this.... If you discover that it just isn't fun trying to manage a large business, then pack it in. Find a buyer and go on to the next thing.

There's nothing that says you have to keep going when the going no longer brings satisfaction. Do what your heart tells you that you should do.

The smartest thing to do, is to include an exit strategy as part of your initial business plan. Figure out what you want to accomplish. Decide how much is going to be enough. Have a plan to sell the company and move on, when you first get started.

An alternative strategy would be simply to find the level of business that you are happy with, and then maintain revenues at that level.

If being an entrepreneur is the thing you most enjoy, then don't stick with any business past the point where the need for an entrepreneurial mind-set begins to be replaced by common management skills.

However, if the idea of managing a multi-million dollar company has great appeal for you, then don't let anything stop you. Just learn about the barriers that stand in your way and come up with a plan to soar right over them. Learn about shortcomings that would limit the success of your expanding business and then take steps to overcome them.

What's required to grow to the next level?

The following questions will help you understand what levels of growth you would find sustainable and satisfying:

1. What are the annual revenues of your business at this time?
    $_____

2. How big a business would you like to manage?

    Make a selection from the following choices:

    a. I'm making the right amount right now.
    b. I want $100,000 revenues per year more than I'm currently taking in.
    c. I want $100,000–$500,000 revenues per year more than I'm currently taking in.
    d. I want $500,000–$1 million more than I'm currently taking in.
    e. Unlimited

3. If you selected **a** or set any upper limit on the upper size of your business, then what will you do? (Select one from the list.)

    a. Control growth to remain at the ideal level.
    b. Sell the company when the right level of revenues is reached.

4. If you selected **d**, then you have to do some serious plan for the following:

   a. Develop skills and abilities to manage a large, complex organization.

   b. Find a leader of a larger company in your field and ask to spend some time in a mentoring relationship with them.

Principle #18 - Learn New Paradigms

Nobody ever became wealthy through their own efforts without learning to look at things differently than the average person would. After all, if the elements of success were obvious, everyone would be finding them.

You have to learn out-of-the-box thinking. Learn to leverage negative things as positive. Have the attitude of the person who said, *If life hands you lemons, call me. I'll bring the rum and salt.* Let's not simply accommodate ourselves to change, let's figure out how to celebrate!

Once again I can illustrate this from personal experience with my agriculture business. Not all the changes in our Northern California community have been good for local farmers. Just the opposite. Most obviously, area farms are losing land to developers. For example, local residents are enthusiastically welcoming a new outdoor mall, but in creating that new development, construction workers have poured concrete and erected buildings on 60 acres of what used to be rich bottomland, and have thus removed the soil from production forever.

A common occurrence witnessed by all of us residents is driving by a field and seeing rows of trees lying on their sides where a thriving orchard had been only the day before. There was no point in the grower trying to make a meager income off those pistachio trees, for example, when a huge Lowes was willing to pay so much money to erect a giant shopping center in order to compete with the enormous Home Depot that had been erected right across the street only two years before.

Another driving force behind the loss of land is the growing instability of small mom-and-pop farms. It has become increasingly more difficult for a farm family to eke a living out of a few dozen acres of farmland

and, as a result, over the past 30 to 40 years many smaller farms have been smothered by the encroachments of malls and sub-divisions, some of them following decades of planting and harvesting.

In other cases, larger commercial-based industrial farms are enveloping smaller farms so that more and more local agricultural production is being generated by fewer and fewer farming enterprises. Even the larger businesses are struggling to survive.

Besides losing the land itself, our local area had lost nearly its entire agricultural infrastructure. The elevators, packing plants, and farm supply stores that in the past formed a major part of our local economy are all gone.

When a fuel pump fails on one of my tractors somebody has to drive a 50-mile roundtrip in order to get a replacement part. And, of course, if in replacing the fuel pump it becomes apparent that an associated gasket has also failed, then we have to once again make the same round trip.

If current trends continue unchecked, then farming towns are clearly destined to lose their economic stimulation forever and the areas will finally end up as patchworks of home subdivisions, car dealerships, and fast-food restaurants.

The challenge facing us is to learn how to thrive because of the changes and not simply to survive in spite of them. We will learn new patterns of conducting the business of farming. We will specialize. We will no longer attempt to force the new wine of our changed farming environments into the old wineskins of a deadly *business as usual* approach to our profession.

In particular, we will stop running our farms as purely commercial enterprises and will orient our business to a more local retail model. We will begin conducting direct sales rather than depending upon giant wholesalers to pay us enough for our products to keep us in business.

Some farmers are currently finding the change difficult to make, but unstoppable forces of agricultural globalization and industrialization are driving our local agricultural economy, so we need to push for a stake in our local marketplace to keep us going and to maintain our reputation of agriculture excellence. The big challenge is to secure for the small farmers in our area the type of support they need over the next ten years to enable them to transition into the changed environment.

The opportunity is actually huge because the fact is that only in single-digit numbers are area residents buying products from the local farming community. Local consumers are an untapped market profile that we have only begun to work on.

The majority of the product we are selling ends up on breakfast and dinner tables located far distant from our fields and groves. If we channel the thinking of local residents into buy-locally habits, they will become an economic force powerful enough to support our current local farmers, plus lead to the creation of the additional micro-farms and boutique type agricultural programs required to meet the rising demands for our local agricultural products.

By altering their thinking—changing their paradigms—farmers would generate a lot more revenue for themselves while the residents would reap the benefits of having access to superior and fresh local produce.

Where can I apply new paradigms?

The following questions will help you find paradigms:

1. Read your business plan carefully. What processes, markets, or sales techniques strike you as commonplace and boring?
   Think of two other replacements you could make for these.
2. List on a piece of paper as fast as you can 10 ways you could improve your business.
3. Go back over each of these and sort them out into three small lists labeled *bad*, *good*, and *best*.
4. Throw away the *bad*, file the *good*, and make plans to implement the *best* ideas.
5. Repeat the four steps from time to time. Learn to make a habit of thinking outside the box.

Principle #19 - Learn to do Business as *UN*-Usual

One of the key requirements in the modern world is to thoroughly grasp current marketplace realities. I'm succeeding in a number of business ventures because I understand that this isn't my grandfather's marketplace and I'm not practicing my grandfather's business methods.

We can't employ business models in this Twenty-First century that ensured success in the 1960s because revolutions in technology and communications are changing everything. The burgeoning power of the Internet combined with the surging forces of globalization means that we can't conduct business in the same way we did even a decade ago.

This is a marketplace for young energetic entrepreneurs—or at least for those who are young at heart. Financial success is reserved for people who are fitted by attitude, temperament, and training to compete as businesspeople in this new season.

More than two-thirds of all businesses fail within the first two years and the most common reasons for their failure lies in the lack of know-how for launching business. Competing successfully in this dynamic world requires energy and preparation.

Individuals come to me all the time with what they consider to be exciting new business opportunities. Because they've thought of a business and have come up with an idea and a name for their new enterprise, they believe thereby that they are ready for their first customer. They will almost certainly fail, however, because they haven't even begun to get ready to launch a successful business. Coming up with a seemingly good idea and a catchy name doesn't even get you to the starting line; you're still in the locker room.

Nolan K. Bushnel, who came up with the ideas both for the Atari Game Machine and for Chuck E. Cheese Pizza-Time Theaters, once observed that anyone who took a shower had one of these *good ideas*. The fact is you can't even tell if the idea is actually good or not without a lot of effort. Actual profitability lies at the end of long hours, possibly months, of discipline and planning.

In the absence of careful planning, sufficient resources, and the right people, any business venture is simply a house of cards destined to tumble at the first puff of wind that comes along. No business will ever become successful without developing a well-thought-out plan that identifies in detail all the facets of the new business.

Even though starting a business in this modern environment is difficult, it doesn't need to be risky. Or at the very least, the risks are clearly defined. I never have to second-guess my business decisions.

I formulate a business plan that does a thorough job of identifying such things as the new organization's sources of finances, vendors, suppliers, customers, the required level of performance (both long and short-term), profit margins, competition, resources, marketing strategies, etcetera. I don't have to do any flying by the seat of my pants or hoping for the best.

All that is required is to simply implement on the plan. As a result, success is still not easy, but with such a detailed roadmap, the process is relatively simple because it lacks the confusion and unrealistic expectations that sink so many new business ventures almost before they begin.

By overcoming limitations, understanding resources, learning strategies, establishing tactics, incorporating accountability, and instituting planning by which we can march into the future with confidence, we do *business as UN-usual* and we will ultimately succeed at whatever we do.

What would *business as UN-usual* be for me?

The following steps will help you develop an unusually excellent business venture:

1. Put a lot of thought and care into your business plan. Be sure to cover in detail markets, vendors/suppliers, clients/customers, personnel, products, plans for compliance with government regulations, bookkeeping tasks, quality control, payroll.
2. You can often get step-by-step instructions or guidelines from the local Chamber of Commerce.

3. Ask local trusted businesspeople to give you advice.

4. Do research on the Web. For example, a Small Business Planner section on http://sba.gov offers a lot of help on doing the business plan itself.

   http://myownbusiness.org is another helpful-looking site, with online classes available to help you confront the challenge of doing business as *UN*-usual.

Principle #20 - Never Cease to Learn

I'm a life-long learner. Every day I learn new things. I'm always anxious to figure out what else I can learn that will help me succeed. Political theorist Benjamin Barber made a great observation:

> *I don't divide the world into the weak and the strong, or the successes and the failures, those who make it or those who don't. I divide the world into learners and non-learners.*

I heard the story of a county farm agent who visited a farm and found the farmer sitting in a rocking chair on the front porch of his house.

"Hello, Farmer Brown," the agent said. "I've come to help you learn how to farm better."

"Ain't interested," Farmer Brown said.

"Come now," said the agent, "Wouldn't you like for me to tell you how to farm better than you are farming now?"

"Nope!" said the farmer. "Because I already know how to farm better than I'm farming now."

People with that kind of attitude—and I run into them all the time—are beyond help or remedy because they don't want to be helped, on the one hand, and because they don't understand what needs to be remedied, on the other.

Many other small businessmen really do want to learn to do their business better than they're doing it. They are frustrated and upset by their inability to move ahead. They are struggling with what they know are their inabilities to succeed at high levels.

A large part of my success is that I'm always in a learning mode. I'm in a position of reflecting upon the things that happen to me and learning from them. Learning from experience requires a particular mental attitude. C.S. Lewis wrote, *What we learn from experience depends on the kind of philosophy we bring to experience.* This means that we are required to bring to experiences a spirit of philosophical reflection that enables us to draw lessons from them and then adjust our behaviors and decisions in the future.

We can also learn from the experiences of others. I learn things from my children, from my wife, from my neighbors, from the people working for me. I learn from my competitors, also asking myself, *What do my competitors know that I haven't yet discovered?* The greatest learning of my life was from the mentorship of competitors who owned similar businesses.

An old proverb says, *If a man knows and knows that he knows, he is wise. Follow him.* Search for those wise men and women. Develop relationships with them. Meet them for coffee periodically. Listen to what they say and keep your mouth shut about your own opinions. This is about what they know and not about what you think. Try out ideas on them. Get their opinions, but don't make the mistake of letting them make decisions for you. You need a mentor not a master.

Learning comes to us as a natural result of not always trying to take first place in every relationship or social situation. A wise person can learn from social or even intellectual inferiors. George Herbert Palmer, a noted Harvard professor, said, *I am defeated and know it if I meet any human being from whom I find myself unable to learn anything.* This type of learning is barred to arrogant people. They wish to speak and to instruct rather than to listen and learn.

Develop the life-long habit of reading journals and magazines that keep you abreast of things that are happening in the world, especially as they have to do with your business. Strive to become an expert and to maintain your expertise. Become one of those wise people who *...know and know they know* that we just spoke about.

Shut the TV off. Treat dramas and especially Reality TV as guilty pleasures. Stay away from them as much as you can. Spend your evenings reading and researching. Invite people to dinner who you can learn from. Watch documentaries; listen to National Public Radio (NPR) on your radio.

I seldom go to bed without realizing that during each day my eyes were opened to truths that I had never before imagined; I had learned things that I never knew before. Such learning changes us. The noted jurist and poet, Oliver Wendell Holmes, made an accurate observation when he wrote, *Man's mind stretched to a new idea never goes back to its original dimensions.*

Hopefully you understand what I'm talking about and are prepared to pursue the kind of in-life and life-long learning that I'm describing. A lively curiosity about the world and an intense wish to understand the nature of human existence, including how the world around us works in all its dimensions, is a hallmark of intelligence and a requirement for excellence in business.

If possible, plan to learn five new things each day, until the day you die. The joys associated with discovery and learning, all by themselves, carry their own rewards.

How can I maintain life-long learning?

The following activities will help you maintain learning as a life-long activity:

1. Record in a log or journal every day of the things that you learn. A great deal of success depends upon us remembering information and lessons that we've learned so that we avoid the curse of those who *forget history* and so *are doomed to repeat it.*
2. Subscribe to one or two top journals in your field and read them carefully.

3. Read the newspaper standing up. It isn't worth spending enough time in it to sit down.

4. Spend a couple hours a week in purposeful-not-structured surfing on the Web. Learn to check Wikipedia.com for topics you wish to learn about.

5. Structure your TV watching. TIVO or DVR programs that will actually inspire you and teach you something.

6. Get into the habit of doing these things.

7 Principles About Relating with People Successfully

People can be the most frustrating part of your business, but without a doubt they are your most important asset.

The difficulty with people is that they simply do not behave themselves according to the standards of behavior that we would expect of them. They almost always let us down. But we shouldn't let that bother us. As we admit in our more honest moments, we let ourselves down.

Be not angry that you cannot make others as you wish them to be, said the great medieval mystic, Thomas á Kempis, *since you cannot make yourself as you wish to be.*

We can put up with difficult people by realizing we are difficult ourselves. I've had more trouble with myself than with any other person on earth.

We are all part apt to do things that are confusing and disruptive. The movie producer, Nora Ephron, wrote, *Insane people are always sure that they are fine. It is only the sane people who are willing to admit that they are crazy.*

We must put all that behind ourselves, realizing that people are going to be difficult, and then just get on with the tasks of working with them.

The following pages describe some specific ways of making your connections with other people work positively for the good of your business.

The biggest asset great leaders have is the intangible ability to deal with difficult situations and difficult people. If you cannot do this, the road to success will become long and arduous.

I could write an entire book on what it takes to influence the people that impact our business. In short, when dealing with difficult people or employees, focus upon your real purpose—to be successful by serving others and creating win/win situations. That will contribute to everyone's goals. Once others come to trust your intentions they will cooperate in achieving the shared success that you are working towards.

The following pages contain important principles that will help you become the business leader, employer, and businessperson that your clients and customers need you to be.

Principle #21 - Pursue Humility

The first and most important relationship you can get straight is with yourself. Only by recognizing the truth about yourself, you will then be able to relate well with others. Many young entrepreneurs who are seeking only to become millionaires miss the important role that genuine humility plays in making them successful.

First, we need to recognize the limits of our knowledge and abilities. The great social commentator, G. K. Chesterton, once observed that, *The men who really believe in themselves are all in lunatic asylums.*

Of course, any success we can experience requires a measure of self-confidence, but arrogance pushes self-confidence into an unhealthy realm.

Far better is to follow the advice of the English Peer, Lord Chesterfield, who said,

> *Never seem more learned than the people you are with. Wear your learning like a pocket watch and keep it hidden. Do not pull it out to count the hours, but give the time when you are asked.*

Humility has gotten a bad rap because it is mistaken for the odious, repellent, and shallow self-effacement of false humility, through which some people pretend not to be as good as they actually are. False humility is simply a shabby way and ultimately vain technique for trying to manipulate other people's responses. C.S. Lewis maintained that people who feel that they are being humble are actually very proud indeed.

As a matter of fact, true humility is the simple quality of accepting and embracing ones's own gifts and abilities as a basis for recognizing and even applauding the gifts and abilities of people around.

According to Lewis, *true humility is to regard the virtues and talents of people around me with the same delight as I regard my own.* The sign of a truly humble heart, Lewis said, comes when I imagine myself to be surrounded by wonderfully gifted and admirable people. He wrote:

> *Do not imagine that if you meet a really humble man he will be what most people call 'humble' nowadays: he will not be a sort of greasy, smarmy person, who is always telling you that, of course, he is nobody. Probably all you will think about him is that he seemed a cheerful, intelligent chap who took a real interest in what you said to him.... He will not be thinking about humility: he will not be thinking about himself at all.*

Accepting my true position in life and the abilities that I have equips me to then learn from people around me who are better than I am in some area and thus to regard other people as sources of learning and improvement.

We reach the most important part of humility at those times when we put ourselves in the service of the people around us. Life does not reach its zenith when I learn to profit from my relationships with others, but when I find delight in serving Heaven and in serving other people whether or not I derive any profit from doing so.

You will limit yourself and your ability to become truly successful if you regard every relationship from the point of view of how you can leverage the relationship for your own advantage and then discard those relationships in which you can't find any personal benefit coming to yourself. People who do this are *users*—and such people will never find success and fulfillment in life no matter how much money they have in the bank.

The safest place you can be in your relationships to others is to be servant to them. I regard myself as a servant to the people working with and for me. No lasting harm ever comes to me from this because a principle built into the moral universe is that the more you give the more you receive.

True humility always excludes manipulation. I can't serve others in order to force my service in some backwards way to work for my profit. The principle works only when we learn to give to others without expectation of return. It's a matter of having our heart in the right place—the place where good things can flow to us.

Jesus said, *Give, and it will be given to you. A good measure, pressed down, shaken together and running over, will be poured into your lap.* And then he explained the underlying principle of reciprocity that makes the thing work, *For with the measure you use, it will be measured to you.*

Note that Jesus is simply stating a universal principle without reference to specific creed or religious tradition.... This reciprocity principle operates as well for atheists as for theists; as well for Jews as for Christians; for Muslims as for Hindus. Worldview doesn't matter. You can think of this as karma. Or you can imagine, as I do, that it is the providential grace of God working on behalf of those who serve Him by serving their fellow man. The fact is that it works.

Putting ourselves into service for others becomes a reasonable choice. We can't do this from a purely selfish motive since the required attitude of the heart will be missing and the benefit negated by our selfish attitude. But we can certainly serve others out of a humble spirit without fearing that we are, thereby, working against our success.

A gifted writer, John R.W. Stott, wrote a stirring passage on such servanthood:

> *People are illogical, unreasonable, and self-centered.*
> *Love them anyway.*
>
> *The good you do today will be forgotten tomorrow.*
> *Do good anyway.*
>
> *Honesty and frankness make you vulnerable.*
> *Be honest and frank anyway.*
>
> *What you spend years building may be destroyed overnight.*
> *Build anyway.*
>
> *People really need help, but may attack you if you do help them.*
> *Help them anyway.*
>
> *Give the world the best you have and you'll get kicked in the teeth.*
> *Give the world the best you have anyway.*

I'm glad to put myself into service for others and every day I give thanks for the fact that a great many remarkable people surround me. My wife, children, friends, people I worship with, and work with are teaching me, helping me to grow, and are continually enriching my life. I would die for them.

This humble relationship of service to others creates the kind of joy-filled life that I want.

The fact that such an attitude is ultimately good for business provides only a secondary reason for such behavior—although the fact that it does so is demonstrably true.

What am I going to do to develop humility?

The following steps will direct you towards an appreciation for yourself and an attitude of service for others:

1. Ask 5 people to make a list of what they consider to be your six best qualities.
2. Put the names of 5 acquaintances and by each of them list 5 qualities that you most appreciate about them.
3. Go to the people you wrote about in the previous step and share with them the good things that you listed about them on your paper.
4. Repeat the three steps above every year. Make a habit of developing and preserving your humility.

Principle #22 - Master the Requirements for Trusting and Being Trustworthy

If people believe that you will keep your word to do what you say you will, and if they have confidence in you that you also have the ability to do the right thing, then they will put their trust in you to do what you say that you will do. Trust will be lost, however, if they doubt either your willingness or ability to do right.

Entrepreneurs pay a tax when trust is lost. *He is a good person but had no idea what to do when that crisis occurred*, and *He has a lot of know-how but he isn't willing to follow through on his commitments*, are the kinds of misgivings—the first having to do with ability and the second with character—that will hold people back from being able to give you the trust that you need in order to be successful.

When I was trying to capitalize my first business the bank officer offered to loan me money in the absence of sufficient collateral because of my track record over the previous two years of running a business in which I always did what I said I would do.

I was a hard worker, willing to put in the effort to make things happen; I had the innate ability and attitude, and I had developed the skills needed for the job. I found a bank officer who was willing to trust me.

Demonstrating integrity, talent, and skill will lead people to have confidence in you. Your personal influence with employees, customers, clients, and vendors will grow along with the reputation that you will develop with these people.

You simply have to make sure you acquire the required attitude and talent before you begin a business. Don't let a foolish dream push you in a direction where your talents could never take you. Talent and skill make an interlocked pair. You could never become a skilled craftsmen if you didn't have the innate talent. On the other hand, if you have the requisite talent, then creating the skills is just a matter of hard work. Developing integrity is simply a matter of always keeping your word.

A friend told me that his world went through a fundamental shift when his wife told him one day, *Don't ever tell someone that you're going to do something and then not do it. It's fine to do something without telling the person you're going to do it. But if you aren't going to do something, then never say you are. If you say you are going to do something, then make sure you actually do it.*

It was profound advice. Successful entrepreneurship, involves taking advantage of opportunities. A high level of trust is one of the internal qualities that really does provide opportunities for you to excel beyond your competitors.

It's amazing to me how many businesses miss the importance of trust. The saying, *The check is in the mail*, has become a byword for dishonest conduct. The person given the message often knows that the sentence is a delaying tactic. He knows that the check really isn't in the mail. And furthermore, in many of these cases, the person giving the assurance knows that the other person knows that no check is in the mail. It is just a bogus technique for reassuring people that eventually they'll get their money.

That's a slip-shod and lousy way of conducting business. It works against the business case for people who do this. Imagine how readily clients or customers would run to a competitor if they knew that they would never encounter such prevarication.

Businesses ultimately flourish both by attracting new customers and by keeping the ones they have. Creating a high level of trust puts the wind at the back of any organization in accomplishing both of those important tasks.

Many of my customers wouldn't even think of looking anyplace else for service or products. They know who I am; know that I'm a man of my word. I'll give them service they can depend upon. If anything goes wrong my people are right there to fix it. My clients and customers tell others about us. Word of mouth is one of my biggest tools for growth.

I can't tell you how many business opportunities I have been able to take advantage of simply because people have come to trust me—to believe in their hearts that I possess the honesty and skill to do what I say that I will do.

The other side of trust is trusting. I'm inclined to trust people in the absence of some indication that they aren't trustworthy. You can do yourself and others a great service by demonstrating trust to them. Nothing moves people more surely in the direction of becoming trustworthy than to have someone trust them.

I've done business with a man who never writes contracts unless his client demands it of him. He told me, *I'm not going to protect myself. If my client wants to roll me over the clover I'll never take him to court.*

I'm not sure how wise the guy is in taking trust to this level, because a contract serves to do more than simply to protect the parties involved. But I am sure that the man's practice of carrying out intellectual property transactions worth $15,000 or more with a simple handshake is moving in the right direction.

I imagine people will sometimes take advantage of him, but then how many people take advantage of us anyway? Any customers, clients, vendors, suppliers, and employees who violate the terms of a contract are often safe from redress. And even when they are not, the tasks involving attorneys, court schedules, process serving, depositions, etcetera are laborious, time-consuming, aggravating, expensive, and often pointless.

Far better in many cases is to just cut losses, sever the relationship, and move on to people who are worthy of your trust. Losing money to unprincipled people and losing it to rapacious lawyers are equally odious to me. And if you run your business from a litigious point of view, the lawyers will end up with more money than you would have lost to the people who took advantage of you.

If you are doing business with someone and are afraid that the person will take unfair advantage of you in the absence of an enforceable contract, consider doing business with someone else.

Being trustworthy and being trusting towards others, will help push you in the direction of success.

How can I become trusting and trustworthy?

The following steps will help you become more trusting and trustworthy:

1. Make a list of the times recently that you didn't keep your word.

    Resolve never again to make commitments or set expectations that you are unable to keep either through carelessness or through lack of skill, time, or talent.

2. Think about your current commitments.... Who is depending upon you now to perform some service or to meet some obligation?

3. Resolve to discharge your duties in these cases to meet or exceed expectations.

4. Think of recent experiences in which someone failed to keep a commitment to you.

    a. Reflect on the disappointment and aggravation the experience caused.

    b. Gently confront the individuals involved, as you have a chance to do so, and enlist them to share in your determination to become trusting and trustworthy.

Principle #23 - Be Smart About Partnerships

Getting into inappropriate business relationships is one mistake that newbie professionals make. An important principle is to never take on a partner, to bring to the table, any service that you could hire someone to perform.

Don't enter into a partnership unless it is absolutely necessary. Think about a partnership as you would think about a marriage. Get ready for a partnership as you would prepare for a marriage. It has all the same ingredients, beginning with a complete and unconditional trust between both parties.

Also, make sure there is a sense of compatibility between you and your partner. Someone said you should never marry someone you wouldn't want to take a three-day bus trip with. The same should go with any perspective partner. If you don't like being with them, just let it go.

Ask yourself what the perspective partner would be bringing to the table. Don't enter into a partnership because of personal feelings of in-security. Sometimes we want a partner simply because we fear facing the unknown by ourselves. We dread the prospect of failing without someone by our side to share the pain with us. Let that go. Trust me, failing can be even more painful when shared as it is when experienced alone. Sometimes failure is much more terrible when others go down with you.

Imagine how things will be after you are successful. It's a year from now; you're making profits; things are going well. But you still have that security-blanket partner that you have to put up with or break up with. That's another thing that's true about partnerships as about marriage. *Breaking up is hard to do.* In both cases it exerts a toll that you will pay for both with grief and money.

One last comparison between partnership and marriage—for some marriages a pre-nuptial agreement is in order, but when you go into a partnership you better have everything spelled out in detail regarding rights, responsibilities, finances, with a buy/sell escape clause for ending the partnership when it becomes necessary to do so; you need an exit plan.

I am not a big fan of partnerships; they usually don't work out. However, healthy partnerships, though rare, can be extremely powerful. Make sure that any partner has *skin in the game*, and is equally yoked to the endeavor in some substantial way, which will usually be financial.

What changes do I need to make in my partnership relationships?

The following questions will help you identify changes you need to make in partnerships:

1. Do you know a person willing to partner with you who could bring resources to your business that you couldn't otherwise find?

    If *Yes....*

    a. Are you compatible with the person? (Would you go on a 3-day bus trip with them?)

    b. Is the individual trustworthy? Would you trust them with your life?

    c. What positive value is the potential partner bringing to the relationship?

    If you answered *yes* to all three you should make a plan for *courting* the person and putting a partnership together.

2. Are you currently in a partnership with someone?

    If *Yes....*

    a. Are you and your partner constantly having troubles and conflicts with each other?

    b. Has your partner given you reason to mistrust their intentions, behaviors, or abilities?

    c. Are you gaining something from the partnership that you would be able to outsource—i.e., are they providing some resource that you could purchase?

    If you answered *yes* to any of the three you should make a plan for *divorcing* yourself from the person and putting the partnership behind you—by one of you buying the other out. Do whatever it takes to get out of the partnership.

Principle #24 - Fit the Right People into the Right Positions

There's no Lone Ranger thing going on with business success; you have to get a team in place. Any successful business requires the services of a team of people with various gifts and personality types. If the people working with me all shared in my entrepreneurial personality type we'd be out of business in six weeks. I require analytical people to do bookkeeping, amiable people for customer service reps, expressive people for sales, and people with leadership skills for management.

One of the most important qualities a successful entrepreneur must possess is the ability to put the right people in the right spot. You must learn how to read people—to pay attention to them and develop the listening skills that will enable you to analyze them and to assess what kinds of business tasks will make them happy and productive workers.

Since ancient times, schools of thought have divided people into four different groups—sometimes referred to as a *four-quadrant model*. Such divisions have ranged from Hippocrates' famous Choleric, Sanguine, Phlegmatic, and Melancholy types through the personalities from the Peanuts comic strip: Lucy, Snoopy, Charlie Brown, and Linus.

These divisions are always approximations since the boundaries are soft, and in the real world we each combine elements of the four types into a totally unique combination that characterizes us and not any other person who ever lived.

Although each of us is unique and composed of different combinations of these types, we all have one personality type that characterizes us most accurately.

My ability to run a profitable business increased greatly when I discovered that everyone I met fit into one of four personality types. I've made extensive use of the D.E.A.A. four-quadrant model, which arranges people into groups according to whether they are (following the acronym):

- Dominate

- Expressive

- Amiable

- Analytical

Definitions for the four traits are based on studies that the eminent psychologist, Carl Jung, conducted at the beginning of the last century. The Myers-Briggs Type Indicator Test (Knowyourtype.com) and Keirsey-Bates Temperament Sorter (Keirsey.com) are popular tests for identifying a particular person's personality type.

Any successful business person these days must know how to discern these personality traits in order to be successful in the task or putting the right people in place.

Every successful employer must, in fact, have all these key traits to some degree in order to create a balanced leadership style in making decisions and managing employees.

This principle has guided me in the important tasks of fitting people into positions calling for the personality traits that each of them has. If you aren't good at doing this, only by chance will you ever get the right person into the right seat on the bus driving your business.

For example, if I'm hiring for a marketing position I look for the Expressive trait to be at the forefront, rather having an Amiable-type person. If I'm looking for a Leader for a senior manager position, I'm looking for a Dominant personality.

One other point about this, if you are considering being an entrepreneur and starting your own business, but you aren't a Dominate type individual, you should think again.

Things really become difficult when you get the wrong personality-type working in the wrong position. Placing a Dominant person in customer service, for example, or an Analytical person into sales will simply create frustrations leading to unnecessary workplace drama and failure. Like any entrepreneur, I had to cultivate the ability to analyze and to understand the type of personality required for a particular job.

We first identify people with abilities that will contribute to our company's success, we then equip them with the tools and opportunities to become successful. No one else can do this job for an entrepreneur who is starting a business with any real chance of being successful. Finding good people and fitting them into the team is the required process for taking a good idea through the infant stages to maturity and profitability.

You find the right people to drive the bus and then you direct them towards your destination. Or, if that image doesn't connect with you, think of entrepreneurs as being like a doctor who wouldn't consider going into surgery without their nursing staff, or a lawyer who would never go before the Supreme Court without a prepared legal team, or a quarterback who would never line up without his offensive linemen in front of him.

When you make a mistake in putting people into some particular position or another, then eliminating a person who doesn't fit into the position is as important as finding the right person for that position. You obviously can't do the second thing until you've done the first.

There's no cruelty involved in removing employees from positions that aren't right for them because it will be ultimately good for such people to get out of positions that aren't appropriate for their personalities and abilities. By letting them go or finding them a more suitable position you give them opportunities to find situations that they will be good for and that will be good for them.

What are my human resources? How can I best allocate them?

The following steps will help you identify the right people to work in the proper position:

1. Make a list of all the critical-path positions in your business.
2. For each of the positions, check the qualities and list the personality type that would fit successfully into that position.

3. Check the qualities against the person who you actually have in each position. If the requirements are too far out of sync with the personality of the person in each case, make a plan for an appropriate replacement.

NOTE: when you make such a change, check the qualities of the person you are replacing and see if you might be able to consider reassignment to another position in your company.

---

4. In each interview session from now on make an assessment of the person against the personality type required for that position.

   Keep notes about the required personality type associated with each position so you don't forget to do this.

Principle #25 - Find the Power in Coordinating with Others

We young entrepreneurs must always be goal oriented. However, we must constantly resist the temptation to focus too narrowly upon our own concerns and upon the challenges facing our particular businesses.

We can multiply our profit-making potentials if we take others along with us on our ride. In that way we become genuine change-agents in our world, improving the economic environment and creating a tide that will lift ourselves as it challenges and improves the economic possibilities for the people around us.

All industries have organizations that provide networking and the Downtown Businessmen's Organization. They bring together business owners and CEOs who are engaged in selling into some market in order to create concerted efforts that will enable everyone together to create economic leverage and energy that will be greater than the sum of the power of the individuals working separately.

Business-to-business (B2Bs) provide the most obvious example of the power of such concerted effort that could potentially work across all industry sectors. The buying power of the big chains and mega-corporations is immense because of their ability to leverage economy of scale to keep their per-unit costs down to a level that mom-and-pop size operations aren't able to compete with. However, if 50,000 mom-and-pop operations will join together to present themselves as a single corporate buying unit then each of the small operations can reduce the per-unit cost of the purchases to a competitive level.

Chambers of Commerce, local associations, and businessmen's organizations are just three examples of small operations working together to everyone's advantage. There are trade associations of all kinds that are made up of entrepreneurs who are working shoulder-to-shoulder in efforts to share knowledge with each other.

Look up online B2Bs that you could join. Find out who the movers-and-shakers are in your community. Learn where the networks are. Find the best of them and commit yourself to helping others be successful and accept their help in becoming successful yourself.

If you find a need then help to create one of these groups yourself. I was one of the organizers of a Downtown Merchants' Association. People acknowledge the role I'm playing in serving the community.

Seek to become someone who other people can lean on for counsel and support. We gain power as we learn to share it with others. When I was running my service business I never imagined what benefits would come to me downstream from teaming up with others.

I was particularly rewarded through helping others. If one of my competitors needed advice, I would give it to them freely. If competitors needed their trucks fixed, I would perform the repairs. My company, by that time, had a lot of resources to help the little guy out, and I was willing to share them.

I knew I was playing with fire because these guys were, after all, competitors. What outweighed my fear was a belief that I was put on earth to help people. Doing what you are supposed to do rarely leads to long-range loss. On the other hand, in my experience, entrepreneurs who only wish to serve themselves last about 3–5 years. They always end up working for their business and burning out.

A shake-up came in my industry and because I was good to people, I became their first choice when they wanted to sell their companies. I bought out over a dozen companies this way. I had built up the trust needed to make everyone feel comfortable; the owners knew that I would give them a fair deal and take care of their people. The acquisitions were easy for me. My overhead was already in place; I simply added their customer base. In that way I increased our profits 30–40 percent above what we would have done through simple processes of growth. Not all situations will turn out like this, but there will always be built in goodwill when you are a selfless leader in your industry.

How can I join with others for promoting mutual success?

The following steps will guide you in joining with others to increase the power of your own economic success:

1. Talk to other local businesspeople and entrepreneurs about the networking groups and trade associations they belong to. Ask about the impact the particular association has had on their business.

2. Explore the Internet to find associations that relate to your particular industry.

3. Find the most successful local person in your area and ask if you can associate with them.

   You might be put off by the possibility of being rebuffed. Why would such a person reveal the basis for success to a competitor? However (besides being flattered), many such people—since they are successful—understand the power of the principle we're talking about and would understand the power of cooperating with you to the advantage of both businesses.

   (And if you are rebuffed, don't take it personally. Sometimes we allow hyper-sensitivity about such things to interfere with our ability to push forward.)

4. Permit others to learn from you.

5. Help people who are in trouble.

Principle #26 - Praise for Performance and Loyalty Goes Farther than Pay

I avoid being a boss; I'm serving my people with the realization that the best chance my businesses have of being successful is for all the members on my team to feel that they are successful. People need to understand that their work is worthwhile before they will ever be motivated to put in their best effort.

All real work has intrinsic value. Voltaire observed that work saves us from three great evils: boredom, vice and need. There's also an outward dignity in hard work. There's a noble quality in doing good that is often overlooked. For those of us who are people of faith, work even assumes a sacramental quality spoken of by Martin Luther:

> The maid who sweeps her kitchen is doing the will of God just as much as the monk who prays—not because she may sing a Christian hymn as she sweeps but because God loves clean floors. The Christian shoemaker does his Christian duty not by putting little crosses on the shoes, but by making good shoes, because God is interested in good craftsmanship.

Sigmund Freud made a ringing assertion about work that all employers and employees should understand.

No other technique for the conduct of life attaches the individual so firmly to reality as laying emphasis on work; for his work at least gives him a secure place in a portion of reality, in the human community.

And, I would always add that the words *Work also gives him a secure place in his company.*

Even more to the point, President Coolidge said, *Work is not a curse; it is the prerogative of intelligence, the only means to manhood, and the measure of civilization.* And then he added, *Far and away the best prize that life offers is the chance to work hard at work worth doing.*

An employee in my pest control company said to me years ago, "I'm just spraying houses. It's not important."

I told him, "You are protecting the biggest investment that 95 percent of people have. You are conserving it against decay. How is that not important?"

We can remember the lesson of the two quarrymen working side-by-side with their hammers and chisels. One was beaten down by his work because he was only carving blocks out of rock. The other was lifted up by his work because he was building a cathedral.

Everyone knows that a doctor's work is meaningful; but entrepreneurs have to understand how important the work of each employee is to the development of the business, and then to communicate that importance to each of their employees.

You can solve the majority of your personnel problems by pounding into people every day that their work is important; if they don't do it with their whole heart they endanger the company's ability to be profitable.

Thoreau gave us the sage advice when he said, *Do not hire a man who does your work for money, but him who does it for love of it.* That's the person I want working for me. I try to promote that attitude among my employees and to impart it to all the other people who work for me.

I have a real passion for delivering good people from the 9-to-5 prisons that some of them are in. Work should usually be fun and always be satisfying. Elbert Hubbard, the American writer, publisher, artist, and philosopher, spoke the truth when he said, *Get happiness out of your work or you may never know what happiness is.*

Actually, I hope my employees get happiness from a lot of sources beside work, but if they only work eight hours a day (and some of them work a lot more than that), imagine how much misery there would be in their lives if they didn't find pleasure in their daily labors.

Ignorant managers and employers believe that workers value their paycheck above all else—and that they will fail to do their work except under fear of incurring the wrath of their employer and losing their job. Such people are unaware of extensive research that consistently reveals that workers value appreciation for their work far above the size of their paycheck and value the admiration of their bosses above money. Nearly 80% of employees who quit their jobs do so because of management issues.

It's only good business to communicate the message to all of our workers that their work is valuable and that their job satisfaction is important. Having a team of loyal and committed workers is as good as money in the bank.

How can I reward performance and loyalty?

The following steps will reinforce attitudes and behaviors on the part of your employees:

1. Be alert to what is happening on your team and don't let a single example of one of your people going beyond the call of duty go by without making some heart-felt response of appreciation.

    Look for excuses to acknowledge exceptional performance.

2. Don't usually reward performance and loyalty with bonuses or valuable gifts. Not only are expensive rewards less effective than displays of genuine appreciation, but they are apt to lead to expectations of financial reward on the part of team members that you really need to avoid.

3. Build team-building events into your schedule and budgets.

    Besides whatever training plans you have, schedule some times to reward the team with weekend getaways or day-trips. For most of these, leave spouses and significant-others behind.

4. Write the above three tasks down somewhere as a reminder to yourself. Make a habit out of rewarding loyalty and performance.

Principle #27 - The Better Way in Relationships

I'm not a boss; I'm serving my employees as well as my customers. Every person who works for me has a higher purpose and calling in life than simply making me successful. I stay away from zero-sum games, in which I gain advantage only through someone else's loss. If I'm not looking at a win/win then I'm going to just let the deal go.

The other thing I do is to avoid confrontation. I'm never defensive. Nothing is ever accomplished by striking back and getting even with people who hurt or offend me.

I read an essay once, called *Spitting in Elevators*. Two men were riding on an elevator. The car stopped at a floor and a third man got on. He walked up to one of the passengers, deliberately spat on him, and then got off at the next floor. As the man wiped off the saliva with his handkerchief, he showed no sign of anger nor gave any indication that he had found it in the least disturbing to have another person spit on him.

"What's the matter with you!" shouted the other passenger. "How can you just let another person do something like that to you without getting upset?"

"That guy has great problems," the man answered. "I'm unwilling to let him hand off any of his issues to me nor grant him the ability to disturb my serenity."

Without any doubt there are angry and malicious people in this world. Sometimes out of pain that perhaps came from a terrible upbringing, or out of a response to a real or imagined slight on my part, people will sometimes turn on me and behave in an offensive and derogatory manner.

Of course, my impulse is to strike back—and to make the person pay for their attack. The angry response is easy because I'm just doing what comes naturally. Retribution seems to be a worthy goal; vengeance appeals to our wounded pride; we simply want to get even.

All those kinds of reactions, however, diminish us as human beings. We need to learn to develop a serenity that is impervious to any kind of attack simply because we don't wish to be upset and have made a decision not to let any person's dysfunctional behavior spoil our enjoyment of life. We don't want our blood pressure to rise. We don't want feelings of hatred, anger, and animosity to fill our hearts.

I don't want to have a relationship with any one on the planet that would cause me to want to avoid them. My goal is to never have a single person in my life whom I wouldn't be glad to see at a party or just walking down the street.

I don't want any enemies. I'm in direct competition with some people, but even with them I wish to be *frenemies*, to use a new word circulating around these days. I'm willing to be absolutely corrigible and friendly with them on one level while competing with them for market share and customers on another.

There's no way to get all people to like me no matter how much generosity and love I show to them. (Look at Jesus, for example.) I believe any need to be loved is a social or psychological illness. But what I want to do is to have any sense of anger, enmity, or hatred to always be one-directional. I want an indomitable spirit of grace that will never harbor those dark feelings for another person.

The Bible says that Jesus left us an example so that we could follow *in his steps*. Part of that example was *When they hurled their insults at him, he did not retaliate; when he suffered, he made no threats.* Kipling held up the virtue of

> ...being lied about, don't deal in lies,
> Or being hated, don't give way to hating...

Not only do negative feelings create barriers between ourselves and the kind of life we want to enjoy, they also impede our ability to do business. If I strike back with anger at any person, that person, obviously, will never be a customer or client.

Even worse, their circle of relatives and close friends will never be customers or clients. My goal is to imitate the great accomplishment described by Edwin Markham in his poem *Outwitted*.

> He drew a circle that shut me out—Heretic, rebel, a thing to flout.
> But love and I had the wit to win: We drew a circle that drew him in!

This is a good way to live. And it is a way that increases my ability to do business. People want to be in a business relationship with me. They know that I'm willing to trust them. They know that I'm willing to like them and will certainly respect them.

Who wouldn't want to do business with a person who had that kind of attitude?

And here is one of the most effective secrets of creating positive relationships with people that you can ever learn. A powerful but little-noted truth about human relationships is that if you treat someone you're having difficulty with in a friendly manner, the acts of showing kindness will change your feelings towards the person.

A man decided to divorce his wife. He had feelings of deep resentment and even hatred for her. His friend told him that the woman would be glad to get rid of him.

"If you want to really make her sorry to see you walk away," he said, "then pretend you really love her. Talk sweetly to her. Bring her flowers even when she isn't expecting them. Rub her back before she goes to sleep. Let her pick out the channels on the TV to watch."

And then the man added, "If you do that for a few months, you'll have her eating out of your hand. Then when you leave she'll cry about your going. You will have your revenge upon her for the awful way she's been treating you."

It sounded like great advice so the man put it into practice.

A year later he met his friend again. The friend said, "How did the divorce go? Was she sad to see you go?"

"See me go!" the man said. "After I did all those things we fell more deeply in love with each other than ever before. I wouldn't think of leaving her! I love her with all my heart. And she loves me."

If you're married try this. It's powerful beyond your imagination. And you can use an analogous approach with anyone. Just treat everyone as though they were beloved friends. Feelings will almost always follow the actions.... Even the most difficult person you know has someone who appreciates them; you might as well join the group, however small.

How can I begin to follow this better way in my relationships?

If you do them faithfully, the following simple tasks will transform this area of your life:

1. Write down on a sheet of paper the name of one person who you have hard feelings towards.

2. Next to their name write down three things that you would do for that person this week if they were the person you liked and admired the most.

3. Do two of the things in point #2 this week.

4. Repeat the first three tasks with other people with whom you are having personal difficulties. Make a habit out of being friendly with—and in some cases actually making friends with—people with whom you are having difficulty. The habit will dramatically change your life.

8 Principles About Doing Things That Create Success

We've covered the important basic building blocks of success—becoming successful, learning about success, and learning about creating positive relationships.

Now we come to the most important part—the doing part. This is the point at which *the rubber meets the road*. The following principles will guide you as you take the actual steps that will lead you to success.

We've shown in many ways how important learning and preparation are. But there's a temptation for some people to get stuck at these preparatory stages. A so-called *paralysis of analysis* sets in. The American publisher, William Feather, reminded us that, *Conditions are never just right. People who delay action until all factors are favorable do nothing.*

Business has a rhythm and a cadence. A wise entrepreneur will sense when the right time is to actually start working.

Be prepared but don't over-prepare. Some things you can only learn by doing. Jim White, a sought-after corporate coach and trainer, cautioned us against allowing perfection to interfere with what's actually possible. He made the wise observation, *Everything worth doing is worth doing badly at the beginning*.

So here are the principles about what you can be doing to ensure success.

Get ready for some hard work.

Principle #28 - Take Care of Yourself

Much of this principle may make some uncomfortable or you may just not agree with it all together. I would suggest to you to do something that a good friend of mine often suggests to many of those he leads in studies. It is like eating a fish, you eat the meat and spit out the bones. The most important thing you can do is to take care of yourself. Mark Twain wrote, *Be careful about reading health books. You may die of a misprint.* The fact is that we don't have to study health or healthy living; we simply have to exercise a little common sense.

Many of us entrepreneurs are sleep-deprived, but the benefits of good sleep patterns are immense, not only to health and attention spans, but also arguably to longevity and intelligence.

If you get 6–8 hours of sleep a night, rather than 4–6, you'll be cutting into the hours available for you to work, on the one hand, but, on the other hand, because you are more alert you will increase your productivity. You will work less but accomplish more. And, not of least importance, you will feel much better.

Issues of healthy living have always been important to me. I'm passionate about good health even during difficult times when my health and eating habits seem to go by the wayside. I'm staying healthy myself and creating olive oil products that will enable others to remain healthy. Just as importantly, my daughters eat healthy and, by our example, have come to enjoy, in appropriate amounts and ratios, the fruits, vegetables, seafood, and meat that belong to a healthy diet.

I'm swimming against the current on this because we are a society that is moving too fast and exercising too little. Some of us are not merely snacking on such things as Twinkies, but are eating processed food for breakfast, lunch, and dinner. We're running on fast food, which is easier to get on the run and more available. A couple of Pop-Tarts for breakfast, a soda and a Big Mac for lunch, and three slices of pizza for dinner together with a couple beers.... Who's got time for anything more elaborate than this? Even those of us who don't eat fast food can get processed foods as easily in Denny's as at a KFC.

In *Death by Supermarket*, Nancy Deville spoke about how we Americans are killing ourselves with food substitutes. She subtitled her book *The Fattening, Dumbing Down, and Poisoning of America*.

We're replacing our traditional real foods with mere products, which are processed, convenient junk foods and eating *industrialized foods*, which are comprised of animal-based products that are produced in factories.

You would be better off eating the containers of some food products being sold than to consume the contents. You would at least get some roughage and fiber in your stomach. Cockroaches will thrive on the cellulose in cardboard but disdain some of the processed foods that the box might have contained. If roaches won't eat something, we should probably stay away from it ourselves.

There's a connection between a good diet and clear thinking. We're all better off eating real food; by which we mean anything that in natural ways can be picked, gathered, milked, hunted, or fished. In other words, real food includes organically produced meat, fish, dairy, poultry, vegetables, fruit, grains, legumes, beans, and nuts.

A phenomenon called *hysterical hunger* refers to a syndrome that's been documented in starvation victims causing them to crave and binge. Some people believe that the human body isn't able to recognize manufactured products as real food, so we can suffer from the same craving and binging symptoms as starving people, even though we may be carrying around 150 pounds of excess weight.

The problem is a pressing one. A generation of children are coming up who have never eaten real food, but have all their lives been consuming food products. Obese parents are rearing obese children.

As a result, degenerative diseases commonly associated with aging are showing up in our children. Little kids are getting heart disease, and are being diagnosed at ever-younger ages with Type-2 diabetes.

The problem of processed foods requires each of us to make real choices. Do we want to belong to the diminishing group of Americans who are healthy? Or will we choose to remain with the majority group that is tethered to the health-care system, always overweight but continually dieting, while constantly ingesting a cocktail of drugs that have become required simply to keep us operating at a normal level?

We're eating tons of damaged oils from products and fast foods, Deville wrote. *Saturated fats are stable and you can cook with them better than unsaturated fats. If you expose poly-unsaturated fats to heat or air they create free radicals, which causes heart disease. Saturated fats, on the other hand, contain linoleic acid, which helps prevent heart disease.*

Note that a good diet is essential, but dieting never is. Eating healthy and getting sufficient sleep will serve to keep your weight under control without you having to go on some demanding diet.

Besides that, merely exercise portion control. Don't eat as much as an overweight person would. Learn to control your passion for food. For example, go ahead and eat a piece of pie for dessert. Just don't have seconds. Don't eat pie every day. Don't eat more than three Snickers bars a week. If you do go to McDonald's, don't go every day. And don't supersize anything. If you get a couple things off the 99-cent menu and drink a glass of ice water, you will have eaten as much as a person of normal weight would eat for lunch.

If you drink wine once in a while, only drink one glass. A glass or two of wine is good, they say. Three glasses of wine is bad. In my opinion, no wine is the most appropriate amount on most days. Except on rare occasions, don't drink hard liquor. Alcohol clouds your mind and damages your body. It is bad for you so it is bad for business.

If you are smoking, throw away your cigarettes. Throw them away today! Throw them away now! Throw them away forever! Cigarettes are bad for your health so they are bad for your business.

Don't do drugs; they diminish your ability to think straight. Also, it would be difficult to run your business successfully from behind bars.

A healthy lifestyle based on real food, clean living, and an appropriate amount of exercise will greatly increase your alertness, your attitude towards life, and your ability to live free from medicine—plus it will free you from pain and even increase your intelligence. Joan Welsh, CEO of the Hurricane Island Outward Bound School, declared that, *A man's health can be judged by which he takes two at a time—pills or stairs.*

Do you want to be a success in your life? Start by exercising, sleeping, and eating your way to health.

How will I take care of myself so that I can take better care of my business?

The following rules will help you remain healthy long enough to attain success:

1. Eat healthy: lots of vegetables, plus some fruit every day.

   Grill your food rather than frying it. Eat as much of it raw as you can.

2. Make it a point never to get less than six hours sleep every night. Get eight hours as often as you can.

3. Monitor your food intake. Eat no more than a person of normal weight would consume.

4. Exercise regularly. A half hour a day, 3–4 times a week, is minimum.

   If nothing else, simply walk a half hour a few times a week. The bilateral motion of legs and arms exerts a wonderful effect on your whole body, including digestion.

5. Avoid all drugs and tobacco! Period! Consume alcohol in moderation and avoid hard liquor.

Principle #29 - You Don't Need a Thing to Be Successful

Don't ever imagine that you can't be successful because of lack of opportunity. My own story proves that you don't need a leg up of any kind in order to be successful.

I grew up dirt poor. My mom died when I was five leaving my dad, older brother, and me to manage the struggling family farm. At 18 years of age I was on my own, working multiple jobs and continuing to help my dad keep the farm going.

My life was marked by an inauspicious beginning, but it turned out that the early problems were probably blessings in disguise because they taught me the valuable lesson of self-reliance. I learned to take charge of my own life and destiny. Nobody was going to give me anything so whatever would come to me in life would be because I had learned to unlock the doorway of success.

I had to laugh at a comment by Mike Todd, director of *Around the World in Eighty Days*, who once said, *I've never been poor, only broke. Being poor is a frame of mind. Being broke is a temporary situation.*

Successful entrepreneurs all share in this sense of being in control of one's destiny and never accepting defeat. You can enlist people for wise advice and counsel. You can seek mentoring and support. You can seek avenues of financing through investment contacts. In fact, assembling and marshalling these kinds of resources comprise some of the essential tasks that I've been talking about.

But you can't depend upon these things to make you successful. You can never get yourself into the situation of saying, *If this other person had done this*, or *If only that person hadn't done that, then I would have been successful.*

That's just a lie. You wouldn't have been successful no matter what had happened because you made your success conditional upon other people. Other people don't belong in that position. They can assist you to be successful but will never be responsible either for your success or failure. If you depend upon others to make you successful you will fail every time.

God gave us two ends, someone said. *One to sit on and one to think with.* And then he added, *Success depends on which one you use. Head you win, tail you lose.*

Burt Lawlor declared, *We hold the keys to success within our own hands. Decision and determination are the engineer and fireman of our train to opportunity and success.*

Other people will never be responsible for your success, nor will they be responsible for your failure. You are in the driver's seat; you are the master of your destiny. Your *decision and determination* will be responsible for your success. At least, that's the attitude you should adopt because it is partly a statement of fact and partly a self-fulfilling prophecy—and it is wholly a requirement of people who will certainly be successful.

You can start with nothing in your pocket and end with the world in your hands. It's up to you.

What internal resources will provide for my success?

Consider the lives of successful people you have known or learned about. Many of them, from Thomas Edison to Bill Gates, accomplished greatness by the sheer force of their own "decision and determination."

1. Fill in the blank in this sentence.

   Five years from now I'm going to be earning $_____ per year.

2. How do you plan to get to that point?

   I'm going to create a resource that will bring me wealth by

   _____

   Fill out the line by describing the kind of business or company that you will create, or the changes that you will make in your current business, in order to achieve that goal.

3. On a separate sheet of paper fill out the following:

   The five vital things that I must do today to achieve my goal include:

a.

    _____

b.

    _____

c.

    _____

d.

    _____

e.

    _____

4. Every day replace these five vital things with another list that will be good for that day. Get in the habit of identifying the tasks that are required for success.

Do this every day and you will ensure yourself of success. You won't need anything else. You have it all within your grasp.

Principle #30 - Always Move Towards Your Goal

With this principle we are moving along towards taking responsibility for success that we spoke about in the previous goal.

One reality that I suppose we can all attest to is a loss of energy that sets in when we try to move through life in general, and through business in particular, without a set of clearly-defined objectives.

In the absence of clear goals, someone pointed out that *We become strangely loyal to performing daily acts of trivia*. We find ourselves watching our way through endless stacks of DVDs and reading articles in the *TV Guide*. We don't feel good about ourselves and, in fact, there's nothing to feel good about. We are like sailboats drifting with the vagaries of the wind, or like trucks with engines idling. We're not fulfilled. We're not happy. We're not productive.

Everything changes, however, when we have important and clearly-defined goals in front of us.

I'm a man who is living a goal-oriented life. My reasons for living, like strong roots, stretch deep into the soil of family, business, and community, giving my life content and stability, plus (best of all, perhaps) providing wonderful reasons for getting out of bed in the morning, and running the race set before me each day.

It's impossible to make forward progress without knowing where you are going. We become like the pilot in the old joke, *The bad news is that we've lost power to all our navigation equipment and have no idea where we are; the good news is that we've caught the jet stream and are flying faster than we've ever gone before.*

A well-thought-out goal is the source of a lot of energy, focusing your attention on the activities that will bring success and, even more than that, creating the opportunity for growth and development in your own life as you move towards the things you want.

Pursuing our chosen goals provides us with a journey-inward/journey-outward kind of experience. Because the act of setting, pursuing, and reaching goals carries seeds that produce the harvest of a changed life.

The motivational speaker, Anthony Robins, made a great point when he said,

> *Achieving goals by themselves will never make us happy in the long term; it's who you become, as you overcome the obstacles necessary to achieve your goals, that can give you the deepest and most long-lasting sense of fulfillment.*

The acts of setting and moving towards our goals provide us with protection from the fears and discouragement that confront people who pursue life and business in a less purposeful fashion. None other than Henry Ford made the acute observation, *Obstacles are those frightful things you see when you take your eyes off your goal.*

Jim White, a man renowned for coaching others to success, showed how a march towards goals held the power to accomplish whatever our hearts and minds directs us to do.

From nothing you can accomplish everything, White said, *if you have the will and the heart—so long as you hold yourself accountable to reaching your goals.*

That *accountable* word is important. Every Sunday for the past ten years I write my schedule for the next five days. And then day-by-day I mark my progress against the items on the schedule. I'm accountable to myself for doing these things, and would feel like a failure if I ever left the task undone. Make a habit of setting aside some specific quiet time every week to organize, prepare, and check your progress against your goals.

The more specific our goals are, the greater our chance of attaining them. Psychologist Denis Watley observed that the reason most people never reach their goals is that they don't define them, or ever seriously consider them as believable or achievable. *Winners can always tell you where they are going, what they plan to do along the way, and who will be sharing the adventure with them.*

How can I move myself towards my goals?

Here are three things that can help you move towards the goals you have designed for yourself and for your business:

1. On Sunday evening of each week make a list of all the tasks that you need to accomplish during the week ahead.
2. Schedule these on your weekly calendar.
3. During the week, keep to the calendar schedule as religiously as possible.

   Each day accomplish the tasks and purposes for that day.
4. Do this every week without fail. Make it a habit to live your life driven by your purposes and goals.

Principle #31 - Learn to Leap Beyond Your Limits

Successful entrepreneurs are those who are unwilling to be turned back by barriers that would stop other people dead in their tracks. We succeed as we are unwilling to accept the limitations that others, or even we ourselves, impose.

Helen Keller, whose inability either to see or to hear would have condemned the average person to be disconnected from the world, made a reflection about her own condition that should challenge all of us when she wrote, *I seldom think about my limitations, and they never make me sad. Perhaps there is just a touch of yearning at times; but it is vague, like a breeze among flowers.*

George Bernard Shaw, one of the most successful playwrights in the history of British theater wrote:

> *People are always blaming their circumstances for what they are. I don't believe in circumstances. The people who get on in the world are the people who get up and look for the circumstances they want, and, if they can't find them, make them.*

A perfect example of Shaw's principle happened when I first began running. I joined with a partner who was just a little better than me; we were pretty evenly matched. We would run together. I never got any better even though I was working out every day.

Things changed dramatically when I met another person who was a much better runner than I was. He would actually win races while I was just competing. I began running with this person who was able to run much better than I could. The effort of trying to stay with him during our weekly training runs served to stretch me.

He pushed our running group to move beyond our boundaries. We all began to experience great improvement as, under his influence, we began pushing ourselves to the limit to get better. I moved towards success by changing my circumstances.

Running with that man kept moving me out of my comfort zone.

Writer and entrepreneur Jim White summed up the principle admirably when he wrote:

> *If you are not feeling fear before you do something, it is an indication that the task at hand is not big enough for you. Think of fear as a reassuring signal that you are on the right course!*

As White's quote points out, real improvement comes when we get out of our comfort zone so we can grow. If we want to run with the leaders of the pack we need to find out who they are. Identify the movers and shakers in your community and your industry. Join networking groups. Attend Chamber of Commerce mixers. Appeal to leaders for help and advice.

We should become like the Apostle Paul who wrote, *One thing I do: Forgetting what is behind and straining toward what is ahead, I press on toward the goal to win the prize.*

You will never grow remarkably better until you lose your complacency and begin pushing yourself to the limits of your abilities and circumstances. Only then will you really get good. Pushing against the limits and leaping over boundaries is the path towards excellence.

What appropriate boundaries can I break?

The following steps will help you find boundaries to break and help you break them:

1. List 4–6 things that you think are holding you back from achieving your goal.
2. Beside each one list 1–3 things that you could do, moving out of your comfort zone, to break down that barrier.
3. Look at your list of goals. Can you make these more aggressive? Are you being too easy on yourself? Are you flopping around near the ground when you could be soaring.
4. Go through the first three steps from time to time. Get in the habit of breaking down barriers.

Principle #32 - Don't let Emotions Dictate Choices

Children operate almost entirely on their emotions. Successful entrepreneurs operate their business on a mixture of hot passion and cool calculation. The passion impels us to work toward excellence; the calculation clarifies the directions in which that work should go.

We sometimes fail to achieve our potential because, like children, our passions become mixed with our emotions and we end up doing things that are ill advised or even stupid. The emotions that are most likely to derail our success aren't the noble passions having to do with serving others, striving for excellence, or blessing ourselves and our loved ones.

Wrong decisions usually come simply because we get whiney or vain. We do things that we should have known not to do or we leave undone things that we certainly should have taken care of because of useless emotions such as apathy, complacency, laziness, procrastination, arrogance, or resentment.

For example, research has revealed that many people will turn their backs on an opportunity to make money if they believe that another party will unfairly gain from the transaction. Their attitude could be summarized in the sentence, *Those other people don't deserve to make that income; I'm going to deny myself a chance to earn money just so they won't be able to profit.*

We see that illustrated clearly, for example, when professional athletes go on lengthy strikes in order to gain what they see as their proper share of profits. They obviously know that when they strike for more than a month or two, no settlement, no matter how generous, will ever be able to make up for the income that they lost. But they do it anyway because they feel that the owners shouldn't get that money.

In their minds they're playing a script and telling themselves, *It's just not fair!* The players will prevent the owners from getting that money even if it means that they will lose income themselves in the process.

People in this kind of position feel perfectly justified in their behavior. *It's the principle of the thing*, they will smugly say when confronted by their looney decision. But the situation provides a clear example of emotions winning out over reasonable decision-making.

We ought to make decisions against our own profit, of course, if our actions will harm the environment, for example, or will inflict injury or pain on others. In those cases let's make decisions against our own profitability and say, *It's the principle of the thing*.

But to try to use that argument when the only downside is that somebody else is going to make profits if we make profits ourselves is just childish. Maybe the other party doesn't deserve their profits, but it's stupid for me to give up income of my own just to deprive them. That's the kind of emotion-based actions you expect in a schoolyard.

As a type A entrepreneur I'm often tempted to let pride get in the way of sound decision-making. Passion is a great boost for success, but arrogance creates a barrier to sound judgment.

Anger is the worst kind of emotion when it comes to decision-making; and any show of rage is always destructive. In the 17th century a man named Baltasar Gracian wrote *The Art of Worldly Wisdom*, giving the advice, *Never do anything when you are in a temper, for you will do everything wrong,* which is as true today as when he wrote it.

For my own peace of mind and mental health I need to let go of feelings of anger towards others. Dr. Cherie Carter-Scott, author, life-coach, and motivational speaker, said, *Anger makes you smaller, while forgiveness forces you to grow beyond what you were*.

It is simply good business to be peaceful and soft-spoken to people. Through rage and anger you can sometimes force your will upon others. But force and manipulation are quite different from strength and guidance. You will always remain stuck at a reduced level of success until you can figure out the difference.

It does no good for my employees or associates to see me out-of-sorts and listen to my bad-tempered remarks. I have never accomplished one good thing through any of my outbursts. Forcing employees into some action only because they fear my wrath constitutes a real failure as a manager and leader.

Entrepreneurs will fail if they permit mere passion for starting a business to get in the way of sound financial planning. Keep your feet on the ground; if a business move doesn't make good financial sense then just let it go.

For example: if you are tempted to open the business of your dreams, step back. Don't let your emotions compromise your rational thinking about the project. Create a sound business plan. Don't minimize important issues or overlook factors because of your desire to make the deal happen. Always be prepared to walk away if you can't make the numbers work.

In what ways can I keep my emotions under control?

The following steps will help you keep your emotions in check and to make rational decisions:

1. Step back from a decision and question your motivation.

    Ask yourself if you making the decision is for good business reasons or because of some emotional attachment you might have or some negative thoughts or anger.

2. Try to ask yourself if someone else were making the decision would you consider it to be wise or foolish?

3. If you don't get good resolution, then share the issue with a trusted counselor. Ask the person to put themselves in your shoes and to judge whether you're justified in your decision.

    NOTE: Don't have this conversation with a close friend. We're too apt to take the side of our friends' negative feelings about something—to feel anger, resentment, or greed on their behalf.
    ---

4. If you're still undecided but remain suspicious about the purity of your decision-making process, just drop the matter.

    Always intend to err on the side of wisdom, charity, and grace.

5. When you make a bad decision on the basis of pride or anger, do a post-mortem on the event and resolve to look at similar issues more clearly in the future.

6. Go over the above five steps every time you feel some strong emotion about a decision that you're making. Get in the habit of making decisions as rationally and reasonably as possible.

Principle #33 - Learn to Prioritize

People can't believe how I get all the things that I do done. I'm asked about this every day. There's a simple answer. I prioritize and make lists and schedules of the things that I'm going to do on this particular day; what I'm going to do on the next day. I make rank order lists of tasks so that things that don't get done are those things that are least important.

One thing that irritates me is when people tell me, *I don't have the time*. That's a lame excuse. People who say they don't have enough time simply haven't prioritized their time; they haven't organized their lives.

H. Jackson Brown, Jr., who wrote *Life's Little Instruction Book*, said:

> *Don't say you don't have enough time. You have exactly the same number of hours per day that were given to Helen Keller, Pasteur, Michelangelo, Mother Teresa, Leonardo da Vinci, Thomas Jefferson, and Albert Einstein.*

Guys who attend my weekly studies have asked me, "How do you accomplish so much? Where do you find time for all the things you do?"

I tell them, "You wonder how I can get this done? I'll tell you how you can be as effective as I.... Just turn off the TV. Most of you spend three hours a day watching TV. If you spent that time with your family or your business; you would have 21 more hours of time each week you could spend doing things that actually improve your lives." Watching TV is the biggest time waste for people. Take control of the TV off-switch. Twenty-one hours is a part-time job. If you figure a normal eight hours a day for work, turning off the TV in effect adds more than two-and-a-half days to a person's week. That's huge! If you are 30 years old, by age 65 you could add about eighteen months to your life by simply cutting out an hour of TV watching each day.

As is true with almost every other part of our lives, the ideal principle with TV watching is one of moderation rather than abstinence. Don't get me wrong, I do enjoy watching television; I simply don't spend much time doing so.

Treat this like liquor. If you can't moderate your TV watching, throw that thing in the dumpster. The popular online Real Live Preacher had this to say:

> *One thing is clear to me. You can't know everything you'd like to know. You can't do everything you'd like to do. You can't read everything you'd like to read. You must hold onto some things and let go of others. Learning to make that choice is one of the big lessons of this life.*

Time is the most important resource that any of us has. When you squander three hours on something that does you no spiritual, social, or economic good, you've lost a precious resource that you can never reclaim.

Make it a habit to prioritize, organize, and structure your days and weeks for maximum effectiveness. Find your own best way of doing this. My relatively simple technique involves sitting down each Sunday evening and planning my entire week including daily workouts, business meetings, family events, and other important demands.

For example, if I need to focus on an issue with one of my companies I schedule time to tackle it. Or if a problem is looming on the horizon, I set aside sufficient time to deal with it, thus ensuring that I can deal with the problem in a timely fashion. This in turn enables me to avoid the waste of energy that is often created by our procrastination in unnecessarily allowing problems to become urgent.

Charles Buxton, the English philanthropist, writer, and Member of Parliament, said, *You will never find time for anything. If you want time you must make it.* Planning and prioritizing requires discipline, but the habit pays huge dividends.

Successful people are those who have taken control over their lives and are typically using the minutes in every day to produce a positive effect.

What are the most important things I spend my time on in my life?

Here is a list of tasks that can help you take control over the time resource in your life.

1. Every evening before you leave your workplace make a list of the tasks that you need to accomplish the next day.

2. Prioritize the list, starting with the most important one and moving to least important.

3. Put the items on the next day's calendar—placing the most important first and then downward through the least important.

4. If you run out of hours in the day before you run out of things to do, push the least important items off until the next day.

5. Do this every day. Make it a habit to live each day governed by your purposes and goals.

Principle #34 - Refuse to Accept *No* When You Really Need a *Yes*

No entrepreneurs ever became successful without persistent refusal to accept negative responses from people trying to deny them their dreams.

After making the decision to buy my first business from the two teenagers following the death of their father, as I described earlier (page 48), the big challenge was to secure the funding. With no capital of my own the search for a bank willing to invest in a 21-year-old entrepreneur became laborious. On at least one occasion it was downright humiliating. A loan officer in a bank actually laughed in my face and derided my intention to get a loan.

In 1992 my search for financing finally took me to the loan department run by a dear woman who told me, *We're impressed with your track record over the past two years. You're obviously a hard worker. You don't have sufficient collateral, but we believe in you and we'll give you money.* So there I was—21 years old and owner of my own business that was generating revenues of nearly $100,000 per year.

I was a man on a mission. There was no way I was going to fail to reward that person's confidence in me, let alone fail in my own determination. Within six years I had increased revenues from the business, by more than an order of magnitude, to an annual rate of $10.3 million, which made my little business the fifth fastest growing company in the State of California and the fastest growing in our Northern California region.

The West Region SBA named me Entrepreneur of the Year before I was 30 years old. They threw a big dinner in my honor with a number of local businesspeople in attendance. A particularly satisfying moment occurred following the festivities when an executive from one of the banks who turned me down approached me and said, "If you ever need any loans, let me know."

I told him, "When I was struggling and desperate you guys wouldn't give me the time of day. You actually laughed in my face. I wouldn't borrow from you if you had the lowest interest rates in the state." (I guess I showed a little animosity in the exchange; I hadn't yet perfected Principle #27 - The Better Way in Relationships)

It was a great vindication of my unwillingness to accept a setback—to accept a final *no* when I really did need a *yes.*

Be prepared for setbacks. There's no way that they won't come. However, don't accept them when they do—be prepared to push forward to success. We will never get anywhere without persistence

There are limits to this; when it is time to throw in the towel, don't be stubborn. And don't be afraid to quit something and to go on to the next thing. The bestselling author and public speaker, Anna Lappe, made a mighty affirmation when she wrote, *Courage is saying, Maybe what I'm doing isn't working; maybe I should try something else.*

One of the most important abilities that you as an entrepreneur will be called upon to master is the knowledge of when you should continue to persist and when it is time to pull back and go do something else. Failures will involve making incorrect judgments about these kinds of choices in both directions—quitting too soon and not quitting soon enough. There is a fine line between tenacity that can achieve anything and bullheaded stubbornness that can destroy everything. The worst thing is that you can always depend upon people around you to give you wrong advice in both directions.

Trust yourself. Trust your instincts. If you really do have the right stuff as an entrepreneur you will know with assurance when you should keep plowing ahead and when the time has come for you to shift to Plan B.

How can I be appropriately persistent?

Prepare to follow through on a goal to its end in the face of opposition if any of the following is true:

1. Does the goal you are after affect your core business?

   i.e., would failure mean the loss of the business?

2. Will achieving the goal launch you to the next stage of profitability?

3. Will achieving the goal seriously improve the quality of your product or service?

   Don't mess with quality. *Whatever it takes* should be the slogan you live by.

4. Will the goal materially affect the welfare of your family and/or the welfare of your employees?

Principle #35 - Leverage Opportunities for Success

A large part of my competing successfully in the modern economic system is to simply remain aware of the opportunities around me—to see what is happening and then go for it. This quality of awareness differentiates me from most of the people around me. I am able to see and delineate the opportunity.

It seems to me that the majority of people are asleep at the wheel when it comes to recognizing prospects that are right before their eyes. People are languishing because they are unable to see the opportunities that are lying at their feet.

Stay alert and receptive so that opportunities won't pass you by. Take steps to avoid being swallowed up completely by the details of your business. There must be time for strategy as well as simple tactics. We entrepreneurs have to engage in a continual process of re-inventing ourselves or we're in danger of being left behind by the shifting energies of the always-changing market place.

I allocate mental energy to strategic thinking. I'm always trying to think of how to do things better and searching for opportunities to build my business in new directions.

For example, I acquired a number of properties and was eventually paying a company to manage my rental units. Rather than continually paying a management company to care for the properties, I created my own property management company and, by so doing, turned a continual debit into a profit center that now manages properties for other people—and all my own properties, of course.

My business faced an ongoing struggle finding a reliable source of people to build and maintain the 120 vehicles that we had on the road, so I set up my own maintenance company. I began purchasing equipment from overseas suppliers and set up a business that would build and service not only my own but for other pest control companies throughout the area since they were, of course, having the same problems that we were having.

I grew the vehicle service company into the largest supplier in this region and then sold it off; it is still a profitable enterprise.

My ability to find opportunities for success has led me back to my farming roots, which has become another ancillary and profitable business. The farm has served to create a wonderful lifestyle for our family. And, not least of all, my little farm is making money. It's doing so because I began growing a product that had never before been attempted in my part of the county.

Constant improvement is one of the hallmarks of the successful entrepreneur. Success is never like a plateau, which, once you reach it you can relax and enjoy the wealth that will come rolling to you. Success is more like a trapeze and I'm a flying trapeze artist. I have to reach out and grab for the trapeze that is swinging in front of me. It requires skill and resources to make the leap, to get my hands securely gripped.

However, that's not the end because any trapeze simply provides access to another trapeze out there. I have to make the jump once more, securely grip my hands, and become secure on this new level. As soon as that happens, I can now see the next trapeze swinging back and forth in front of me.

The processes of growth are dynamic and challenging. This is never easy, but who would want it to be? Then everyone could do it. Becoming successful is just hard enough to keep less-focused competitors from succeeding.

What can I do to leverage opportunities?

The following questions will help you find opportunities that you may have been missing:

1. What low-hanging fruit have you not gathered?

   Search for any unnoticed opportunities for expansion that may be right there before your eyes.

2. What economic activities are your competitors and other people in parallel industries undertaking?

Observe the way people around you conduct business and identify opportunities from their behavior that you can copy or even capitalize on.

3. What media opportunities are out there?

   Local media including newspapers, lifestyle magazines, and community newsletters are often searching for interesting copy. Figure out how to make your story interesting and get it to them. It could be not only free advertising, but advertising of a quality that you could never afford to buy.

4. What connections can you still make with people who could work with you or become clients or customers?

   a. Join the local Chamber of Commerce. Attend their meetings. Take your business cards with you and make connections with as many people as you can.

   b. Join a local service organization, such as a Lions Club or Rotary Club.

      Volunteering with organizations such as these will get you good exposure in the community. Plus, fellow members are likely to become customers, clients, or even to work with you in some peer-to-peer project for mutual benefit. Rotary has a slogan, *Rotarians do business with other Rotarians.* It's more than just a line....

Opportunities are all over that you can leverage for your good. You just have to get *out there* yourself and see where they are.

Principle #36 - Practice Frugality

Here is one word of caution about wealth, as you begin to accumulate it. Practice a somewhat frugal lifestyle. Pay attention to the bottom line in your business. The big distinction in our society isn't between the haves and the have-nots, but between people who have sufficient financial resources set aside to maintain them for a while and those who are living from one month's income to the next.

In their book *The Millionaire Next Door*, the authors, Thomas J. Stanley and William D. Danko, reveal what they call *The surprising secrets of America's wealthy*, which is summarized in the principle that if you always spend up to the limits of your income, you will never become wealthy no matter how much you make.

It's amazing how many people—some of them driving fancy automobiles, living in beautiful homes, and taking exotic vacations—are skirting along the very edges of economic disaster. They have maxed their credit limits and if they could ever figure out how to get more credit they would take it immediately and use it up as fast as possible.

Never spend all the money you make. When we started our first business we were maxed. But nevertheless we never spent everything we earned but always set aside a portion of our income—no matter how meager the income was—to replenish a reservoir of funds that we would be able to leverage for our future well-being.

The title of *The Millionaire Next Door* book comes from the fact that most millionaires profiled in the study did not live as extravagantly as their resources would have permitted. They spent only a small percentage of their income on such things as luxurious homes, expensive cars, designer clothes, and flashy watches. The main reason that these people are wealthy is that they live below their means. They were *Balance Sheet Affluent*, to use the book's phrase, unlike those who are *Income Affluent*—having a net worth that was far below their actual wealth.

Buying a smaller home than you could get approval for is the best way there is to become comfortable about your money.

Borrow money wisely—and only borrow money for appreciating assets. Learn to resist the impulse for instant gratification; save money until you can afford to pay cash for your purchases.

Keep a reserve fund on hand for your business. Make it your goal to have sufficient liquidity that you could run the business for three months if you never made a nickel.

Appropriate frugality opens a doorway to real wealth.

What ways can I accrue wealth by appropriate frugality?

The following principles will help you increase your wealth by controlling expenses:

1. Apportion profits according to a principle of thirds. After doing your P & L divide the profits into three parts.

   a. Plough a third in building up your business—paying off long-term loans, making capital purchases, etcetera.

   b. Put another third of the profits into long-term savings in order to build up your working capital, preparing yourself for unforeseen financial set-backs, natural disasters, changes in the market, etcetera.

   c. Put the final third of your profits into your own pocket.

2. Do away with impulse buying altogether.

   If anyone says to you that they need you to make a decision about making some purchase that day, always turn your back on it no matter how attractive the offer seems.

3. Never borrow money to make cosmetic improvements.

   Don't buy fancy desks, window treatments, carpets, pictures, etcetera until you can pay for them out of cash reserves.

4. Look for bargains.

   Larger companies have purchasing agents who are paid to keep costs low on items purchased. You have to be that person. Develop skills at Internet shopping. Do things on trade, when you can. Never pay top dollar. Buy used furniture and furnishings. Never buy electronic equipment from any company that has plush carpeting on the floor.

Principle #37 - Use Synergy to Propel Your Bottom Line

Let's talk about a very important element every small business should clearly understand. Synergy is a tool that should be utilized if feasible in every small company. The definition of this new age term is: when the sum of two equals more as a whole. Three questions we will answer here are:

1. How to find synergy in the business you are in?
2. Why is synergy so important?
3. If I go in to a business what potential synergy can be created?

I am not a big motivational speaker or one who delivers a lot of flash, but it seems all the new business journals and business personalities that come and go, mention terms like *symbiotic, out of the box* or *synergy.* Pick and choose your advice carefully; as an entrepreneur you should learn to discern the difference between flash and trash and a sound idea or concept. Synergy is something, if harnessed and capitalized on can make your business grow and profit beyond what you have ever thought it could. Read and digest this chapter carefully, do not try and blow through it.

When I look at potential businesses I always try to project what incremental revenues I can put on the top of the P&L to flow to the bottom of the P&L. Normally incremental add-on services create great synergy in any business. For instance, let's start simple: Ask yourself what other services your customers are asking for. Listen to them; they are your biggest tool to discover more revenue streams for you to capitalize on. If you run a service-related business like a landscape maintenance company with a customer base of a 1000 clients, are your customers looking for a good window washing company? New construction in their yard? Gutter cleaning services? With those easy add-on services you create more customer loyalty, fewer cancellations, possibly more even-flow in cash flow. If done right you will also create an incremental flow-through of 50% or more to your earnings. Using current overhead and staff are the financial keys to a good synergy plan. Traditional take-rates on the add-on services are over 20% (provided you have good customer service) so the sum of this certainly equates to more as a whole. There are these same relationships in other business types that can also be discovered; you probably already know what they are.

Okay! Let's talk about execution of a synergizing idea you have. This is a very important step that needs to be championed by you as the leader of your company. If you don't have a bulletproof comprehensive initial plan to roll out to your staff, your idea will slowly fail or become an economic disaster. Don't just throw this against the wall and see if it sticks. Make sure you think things through before bringing it to your staff to bounce off of. Get their buy in and articulate your plan, then work out the bugs.

Principle #38 - Move Towards Independence

Entrepreneurs go into business for themselves. The essence of entrepreneurship is to no longer have to work for The Man. Some businesspeople discover, however, that they've just changed masters. Perhaps The Man is gone but his place has been taken by a business that has grown more autocratic and demanding than any shop foreman or district sales manager could ever be.

Such people discover that their time is not their own to spend as they wish. They are not living independent lives, but are, rather, chained to the demands and schedules that the business has imposed upon them. They are working for the business, rather than having the business work for them.

Perhaps that kind of servitude is inescapable during the early days of a business when the tasks of identifying resources, claiming market share, meeting the demands of customers, maintaining relationships with vendors, and keeping the product or service line filled, calls for more time and attention than the new business owner is able easily to supply.

Understand, however, that if you work for your company rather than your company working for you, company growth will be confined within the limits of your own capabilities. When you reach the point of your maximum capabilities—the capacity that you can deal with yourself—then the business ceases to grow.

Too many entrepreneurs get stuck at this point. They've grown their business to a certain level and then stagnate, becoming stuck at a plateau and unable to rise to the next level because of their inability to define where that next level is or what resources would be required to get them to move to that point.

People complain to me all the time about this problem! Things are working, but they're not working well. They are making profits, but are not very profitable. The quality of their lives has declined because the business is consuming all their time and energy.

Every business owner has to face this dilemma and determine whether they want to figure out how to fix the problem or get out of the field and possibly go back to work for The Man in order to get life back.

Identifying and putting into place management resources can eventually overcome this problem. By strategically placing appropriate people, policies, and procedures, business owners automate various activities of the business, in a sense, so that things happen without requiring their constant intervention. Automation of regular rote parts of the business begin to relieve the pressure so that each individual transaction doesn't become a crisis demanding the owner's attention.

The ultimate goal, attained by wise and seasoned entrepreneurs, occurs when the company actually begins working for them.

Not many entrepreneurs are able to move their business to this level because growing a business to the level at which the business begins working for you requires strategic thinking.

This will never happen automatically. Unless you deliberately set aside time and energy to identify your needs and put into place a plan, healthy growth will never happen. You will spend all your time carrying out tactical activities that maintain you at your current operational level and never find time for the strategic planning that will move you into a brighter future.

The goal is to move past the level of running your business, to managing your company by putting into place those people and systems that will cause some parts of your company to run without the necessity of your running them. At least at some points you will know that you are making money even when you are not hard at work.

Many small-business owners will never come to this place. They've got sufficient management processes in place to keep them from going crazy, but they will never move past that into the place where the business is actually working for them. In some cases they are simply content with their current levels. And that's fine. But you aren't at that point or you wouldn't be reading this book.

And you certainly wouldn't have read this book this far unless you really are serious about changing the way you do business.

The cure for finding tyranny from a run-amuck business begins when you identify exactly where you are now so you can come up with a plan to get to the next level. You must become and remain sufficiently flexible to be able to respond to changing circumstances as your business grows, and to control the level of your involvement in the day-to-day activities of the company, securing for yourself a position in which you control the course of your business's activities but are not controlled by them.

Your first step in getting to the next level lies in determining where you want to go so you can take subsequent steps towards your desired destination. When you have done that then you can begin laying strategy. Remember that a comprehensive business plan is imperative to your success. Learn how to put together a measured risk business plan. Then execute!

What aspects of my business are tying me down? How can I untie them?

The following steps will help you achieve the goal of not being controlled by your business:

1. Make a detailed list of all of the tasks involved in your business.
2. Put a circle beside each task that you carry out yourself.
3. Put a check mark beside each task that requires your direct attention.

   Don't be vain about this and imagine that you are the only person who could do a particular task if, in fact, other people could do it—and perhaps do it better than you. In other words, don't check more of these than you need to.

4. Now go back through the list one more time and note all those tasks that have a circle but don't have a check mark.

   These items that you are doing but that someone else could do will provide a starting-point in your quest to free yourself from working for your business instead of your business working for you.

5. Find all the tasks on the list with circles but no checkmarks that you could delegate to someone else in your company who is possibly under-worked.

6. Find the top three remaining tasks that have circles but no checkmarks and that consume the most time and energy. Outsource those activities or hire someone to take these over for you.

   Don't worry about the additional expense; the act of bringing your company into a position in which it really is working for you instead of the other way around will free your mind and probably cause you to be even more effective—and profitable—with those things that you need to be doing.

7. Redo this exercise from time to time in order to make a habit of denying your business the ability to take control of your life.

Principle #39 - Keep Going Back to the Basics

There are only three basic parts of any business. These include the core product or service, customer service, and employee satisfaction.

Many businesses start up, exist or even thrive for a period of time, but end up failing for the simple reason that the people involved have lost track of what they were in business for. Forgetting the basics of the business; and the pieces that made them successful.

Every business has a core service or product line around which the business revolves. When you disturb that you are asking for trouble. Sometimes this happens because leaders become distracted. Restaurants, for example, that are famous for the quality of their cuisine will go into decline when the owners become involved in other activities that draw their attention away from providing the top-notch cuisine that made them famous and profitable.

Schwinn Bicycle Company was the dominant source of American bicycles through most of the 20th century. Schwinn bikes were called the Cadillac of bicycles. However, in the 1980s a new generation of leaders replaced ex-mechanics with MBAs and the quality of the product began to decline. The enormous profits of the past spiraled down into huge losses. The company went bankrupt in 1992, though the name still survives.

It's difficult to maintain superior products and services. Doing so requires continual attention and renewal. But staying focused on the business core—the essential operation for which the company exists—is one of the most important jobs of the entrepreneur.

Customer care is another equally important basic component of a successful business. Present Eisenhower uncovered a deep and abiding truth when he wrote, *We succeed only as we identify in life, or in war, or in anything else, a single overriding objective, and make all other considerations bend to that one objective.* He might have been writing about me; he might have been talking about my businesses. My *single overriding objective* is to provide quality customer service.

The most basic and important element in many of the businesses that I have been involved in is the quality of customer service. I'm passionate about this; I'm pushing towards flawless delivery of product and care accompanied by an attitude of helpfulness and service.

Customer service is inseparable from quality because you will never have satisfied customers if your product is inferior, nor will you ever have contented clients while offering inferior service.

An attitude of *good enough* is never good enough for people who want to drive to the next level of success. Successful entrepreneurship always involves us in a quest for excellence. Bliss Carman wrote, *There is a passion for perfection which you rarely see fully developed but...in successful lives it is never wholly lacking.*

Henry Ford, who obviously knew more than a little about the elements required for a successful business, was writing about customer service when he made the observation: *The man who will use his skill and constructive imagination to see how much he can give for a dollar, instead of how little he can give for a dollar, is bound to succeed.*

The reason for my passion is that, as Henry Ford's comment suggests, customer service is basic to everything else that happens. It is the one great objective that will either lift a given enterprise to great success or will reduce it to a muddle-along level or even to bankruptcy.

As far as I'm concerned, the customer isn't merely *always right*, he is always king or queen. And this should be true whether it has to do with relatively small enterprises like mine or with Fortune 500 Companies.

To paraphrase an old line, originally about mothers, in any of my companies *If the customer ain't happy, ain't no one happy.*

Customer service is the point at which companies intersect most directly with customers. Many of us judge companies on the basis of the way we are treated by their customer service policies and people.

I know a man who has remained a loyal customer of Kodak because of the way he was treated concerning a single camera complaint more than 15 years earlier.

I'm calling customer service *basic* because many companies live or die based upon the level of service they provide. It is not only the most important thing companies do, but it is one of the most difficult; because people are difficult.

Employee satisfaction is another basic area. It isn't a coincidence that companies like Adidas, Nike, and Microsoft all get top rates both in employee satisfaction and in market share. The route to happy customers lies most naturally through happy employees.

These three things—your core business, customer service, and employee satisfaction—are the basics of your business. If you exceed all standards in these three points, you are guaranteed to drive a mediocre business towards the top of its industrial niche.

How can I remain centered on the basics in my business?

You can have the basics covered—and know that you do—by following the steps below:

1. Make a fearless assessment about how high the actual quality of your core product or service is.

    a. Do you really know how good it is?

    Are you collecting any customer satisfaction data?

    b. If necessary consider doing some kind of random phone survey or customer report form to collect information.

    c. Make whatever changes are necessary until customers and/or clients are thrilled by the quality and service they receive from you.

2. Do your employees feel valued and fulfilled in working for you?

    a. Do you really know how good it is?

    Are you collecting any employee satisfaction data?

    b. If necessary consider doing some kind of random phone survey or customer report form to collect information.

    c. Make whatever changes are necessary until customers and/or clients are thrilled by the quality and service they receive from you.

Chapter 8: Principles About Doing Things That Create Success

9 Go and Be Wealthy

The pages you've just read have covered a lot of ground. You have information and challenges enough to drive you to great success. I know these things work because they've worked for me.

Now it's up to you. If you've worked through these materials carefully and thoughtfully you have made numerous decisions about changes you are going to make, attitudes you are going to adopt, and programs you are going to begin.

There's a principle in physics that works in all areas of life, which is that entropy increases. In other words, water always runs downhill. Energy in any system constantly diminishes unless constantly renewed.

The changes, attitudes, and programs that you have resolved to implement will come to nothing unless you keep inputting into the system the energy of your own determination and enthusiasm. In other words, in six weeks you will be right back to the same level of operations that you were at before you began reading this book.

Start making the changes that will bring you to wealth. Every morning begin again to do the things that will bring you success. Make the tasks that will create growth and lead to wealth habitual.

Don't let anything stop you!

About the Author

Sean McCauley is a wunderkind—with the strength and determination to succeed at whatever he does. Sean, a young entrepreneur, was raised in rural poverty and has lifted himself to wealth in the millions through his service, import, and real estate portfolios. The intensity, commitment, and preparation that Sean demonstrates provide practical starting points for anyone who wishes to become wealthy. Though still in his late 30's, Sean has become successful in business several times over, with accomplishments such as SBA's Young Entrepreneur of the Year, and the San Francisco Bay Area's Most Successful Under-40 recognition. He has sufficient self-awareness and analytical abilities to clearly describe the principles and practices that have contributed to his success, so that others can follow where he has led.

To contact Sean please send questions or comments to:
smccauley@mccauleyinv.com.

Create Thought Leadership for Your Company

Books deliver instant credibility to the author. Having an MBA or Ph.D. is great; however, putting the word "author" in front of your name is similar to using the letters Ph.D. or MBA. You are no long Michael Green, you are "Author Michael Green."

Books give you a platform to stand on. They help you to:

- Demonstrate your thought leadership
- Generate leads

Books deliver increased revenue, particularly indirect revenue:

- A typical consultant will make 3x in indirect revenue for every dollar they make on book sales

Books are better than a business card. They are:

- More powerful than white papers
- An item that makes it to the book shelf vs. the circular file
- The best tschocke you can give at a conference

Why Wait to Write Your Book?

Check out other companies that have built credibility by writing and publishing a book through Happy About.

Contact Happy About at 408-257-3000 or go to http://happyabout.info.

Additional Praise for this Book

"As I read through the principles, I think about my last few years as an entrepreneur and can attest that this is a must-read for anyone who is ready to embark on their journey, whether they think they have the DNA or not!"
Jason Alba, CEO of JibberJobber.com, Speaker, Author

"This is not only a practical guide, but a philosophical one. Calling on his own experience at an early age, he has detailed the route to success. You will never learn at business school what is presented in this book."
James P. Neeves, Retired Executive Vice President, W.R. Grace & Co.

"After reading this book, you will find the answers to Becoming, Learning, Relating, and Doing business in a way that is true to yourself, and above all, one that brings you personal happiness and fulfillment."
Linda Lucas, retired VP and Senior Technology Manager of Fortune 100 Company

"Whether you're an aspiring entrepreneur wondering how to grow a business or homemaker looking for ways to better manage your family, set aside some time, pull out a highlighter and get ready to gain some valuable insight from Sean about how to do life with purpose and expectancy."
Ron Bernal, Assistant City Engineer, City of Antioch, CA

"Just retiring after 20 years from a top Fortune 100 company left me questioning my future. Being in corporate America for over 30 years, it wasn't someplace I was in a hurry to get back to. Reading this book gave me a new perspective and a fresh set of dreams. 'DNA of the Young Entrepreneur' is a wealth of information, not only on what it takes to become a successful entrepreneur, but how to become a better you. After reading this book, you will find the answers to Becoming, Learning, Relating, and Doing business in a way that is true to yourself, and above all, one that brings you personal happiness and fulfillment."
Linda Lucas, retired VP and Senior Technology Manager of Fortune 100 Company

"'DNA of the Young Entrepreneur' is a must read for anyone, both young and old, who is looking for some fresh perspective on how to succeed in business and life. Sean gives us a peak into how personal disciplines like the Five F's directly relate to his vision and success in starting and leading profitable businesses. Whether it's growing olives for his emerging oil business or putting in the grueling hours on a bike or running the hills necessary to compete in an Ironman, Sean tackles each new endeavor with a unique passion and intensity. Whether you're an aspiring entrepreneur wondering how to grow a business or homemaker looking for ways to better manage your family, set aside some time, pull out a highlighter and get ready to gain some valuable insight from Sean about how to do life with purpose and expectancy."
Ron Bernal, Assistant City Engineer, City of Antioch, CA

"Being successful is one thing. Being successful because you had a plan and executed it well is still another. Doing that several times is extraordinary. Sharing the lessons you've learned in the process with the world is truly a gift, and that's exactly what Sean McCauley has done with this book."
Scott Allen, About.com Guide to Entreprenuers and co-author "The Emergence of The Relationship Economy"

"'DNA of the Young Entrepreneur' was a very good read...I saw lots of practical applications that I could use in my own business.... There were lots of Wowies that caused me to pause and think about my own situation...now I have to go back and do some of the hard work to bring them to realization! This is a real rags to riches story of a young man who started in the fields and ended up in the boardroom. This is his story, his life, and his own 'pull yourself up by your boots straps' strategies and disciplines. This is written by a young entrepreneur that is still in the battle. As a result, it is a unique and fresh approach that will help you create your own successful story, no matter what your circumstances."
Christopher W. Grow, Certified Public Accountant MBA Finance - U.C. Berkeley, CA

Printed in the United States
130233LV00005B/25-54/P